THE
WEST HAM UNITED
FOOTBALL BOOK
NO. 2

The West Ham United Football Book No. 2

by

Dennis Irving

Foreword by Geoff Hurst

STANLEY PAUL

London

STANLEY PAUL & CO LTD
178–202 Great Portland Street, London W.1

AN IMPRINT OF THE HUTCHINSON GROUP

London Melbourne Sydney
Auckland Bombay Toronto
Johannesburg New York

First Published 1969

This book has been set in Imprint type face. It has been printed in Great Britain at Taylor Garnett Evans & Co. Ltd by offset Lithography in Watford, Hertfordshire

09 097900 1

Contents

Foreword

BY GEOFF HURST

West Ham and England

I was delighted to be asked to make a contribution to the West Ham United Football Book No. 2 as it gives me a chance to say how much we at Upton Park, players and staff alike, were pleased with its predecessor.

The fact that there is a follow-up book is, we feel, a tribute to West Ham as a top club and to our loyal supporters, who are among the best in the land.

In my years at West Ham – and it comes as something of a shock to find myself as one of the senior citizens on the playing staff – I have been imbued with the family spirit that is fostered in the club at director and managerial level.

We aim to entertain as much as to succeed and are old-fashioned enough to retain an emphasis on attacking football. We hope we are good ambassadors for what is the greatest game in the world and also for the good name of a fine club.

Dennis Irving, who I have known for many years now, was co-opted to the West Ham family when he travelled with us to America in the summer of 1963 and shares our attitude to soccer and the good things of the game. Although as a commentator he maintains an unbiased approach, it is no secret at Upton Park that he often lets forth with our 'Bubbles' theme in the privacy of his bathroom!

I wish success to this latest chronicle of our achievements and the stories of some of those who have contributed to making the name of West Ham respected throughout the football playing world.

Ron Greenwood, only the fourth manager in the long history of our club, has said that our burning ambition at West Ham is to win the League championship title so that we can prove our principles are right. Dennis Irving wrote in his last book: 'Let them all play the West Ham way.'

I subscribe to both. I hope we win the First Division title with our brand of soccer so that we can return to Europe and open a new era of prosperity for the Hammers . . . the family club and, to me, the greatest.

I

A-Level in Soccer

Legend has it that a football club manager or scout wanting a player in the 'good old days' whistled down a pit shaft and one appeared.

Gone, too, are the days when a club opened the gates on a Saturday afternoon and a crowd shuffled in, cloth capped and mufflered, having had a pint on the way to the ground after work.

The talk as the 1960s bow out is of a permissive society. The boys of my youth wanted to be train drivers; nowadays the glamour job for most youngsters is that of a footballer.

The country is more affluent and the thought of some of the legendary players of the years between the two world wars earning a maximum £8 a week sounds ludicrous today.

We have progressed at such a rate – the country and soccer that is – that the long shorts worn by the giants of the 1950s provoke laughter from the modern young man.

Floodlights arrived to make football an evening game as well as a Saturday must. Jet travel has broadened our horizons and it is an astonishing thought that barely a decade has passed since authority frowned on Chelsea competing in the European Cup.

The major landmark, of course, was the removal of the maximum wage for footballers – and today a new breed exists. Trevor Brooking is one of the newcomers.

Tall, handsome and articulate . . . well paid . . . much travelled. Trevor and his 1969 counterpart colleagues can mix at all levels and converse on subjects beyond the last game and Saturday's referee.

It is a sign of the times that a soccer writer interviewing Trevor

Brooking is talking to a 20-year-old who has attained 'O' levels in English Literature and English Language.

That's not all. Barking-born Trevor collected seven 'O' levels at Ilford County High School – and another four and an 'A' level in Economic History after he left.

These are the subjects that earned Trevor pass marks at school exam time: English Literature, maths, French, geography, history, chemistry and British Constitution. He failed his English Language test – but later attained that level as well as accounts, statistics and commerce.

All thoughts of a career were held back by the Brooking family until Trevor sat for his G.C.E. examinations but, at the age of 15 when he played football for Ilford, London and Essex as a schoolboy, the football club scouts started knocking at the front door.

'Some of the boys I played with talked of a soccer career and I discussed the possibilities with my parents,' says Trevor. 'We thought it was a bit risky to go into football – to make it worthwhile one had to make the first team grade and not finish an apprenticeship at 18 as a failure, having wasted two years.'

West Ham manager Ron Greenwood arrived on the scene and agreed that Trevor could stay on at school for an extra year to complete his educational programme. Trevor played in the West Ham youth section teams, but not on Saturdays when the school needed him for their side.

Trevor played in the England Boys team of 1963–4 as a wing-half, with W.B.A. inside-forward Colin Suggett and Newcastle full-back John Craggs as contemporaries. He signed as an apprentice professional for the Hammers on 24 July 1965, and as a full professional on 2 May 1966.

'I decided that football as a career was an opportunity not to give up,' says Trevor. 'I had always supported West Ham and at the back of my mind, I suppose, there had always been the thought that I might like to play for them if I was good enough.'

Frank Lampard, the full-back who made the first team grade with Brooking, Roger Cross, Bob Glozier and Barry Simmons, who played in the same Ilford and Essex sides, were starry-eyed youngsters at the same time as Brooking at Upton Park.

If Trevor was good enough. . . . Well, he won six England Youth international caps in 1966–7 and made his first-team début in Switzerland in a friendly match in June 1967 against Grasshoppers. His League début came against Burnley at Turf Moor on 29 August 1967.

Trevor Brooking – one of the modern breed.

Soccer has taken Trevor Brooking to Turkey, to play with the England Youth side in the Little World Cup competition, to Switzerland, the United States, the Bahamas and Italy.

'I've thoroughly enjoyed every minute of it, from the day I made my début as a midfield player and found Ron Boyce and Martin Peters so helpful,' says Trevor.

John Talbut, the W.B.A. centre-half, tackles Trevor Brooking at Upton Park. Notice the empty stand – West Ham did not open up for business until the beginning of 1969.

He is thankful for the inspiration and help his parents have provided. His father, Harry, who played football with the police and was 'quite a good centre-half', and his mother, Margaret, have watched Trevor play since his primary school days. They travelled to Middlesbrough to see him play for England Boys.

Trevor's brother, Tony, a policeman, plays centre-half for Leyton, the well-known amateur club, although he broke a leg last season.

I asked Trevor if he derived inspiration from any other inside-forward or if he had grown up with an idol.

'No,' he replied. 'You go to a lot of matches and you see a lot of different players doing different things. You try them out for yourself on the field, and maybe, incorporate bits here and there. But I haven't modelled my style on anybody.'

It's definitely not a goal. . . . Gurr holds the ball as Trevor Brooking and Martin Peters arrive on the scene. In the background is Harry Redknapp.

What is his role at West Ham? As a striker alongside Geoff Hurst or as a midfield man? Trevor is in no doubt which he prefers – the midfield role.

'Sometimes I have to play up front with Geoff, but I'm not so keen,' he says. 'A front runner has to be nippy and quick – I'm the first to admit that I am not the quickest player. I like a bit of room and, as a striker, I find the defences tight and you have your back to the goal and are playing the ball to oncoming colleagues. In midfield I am facing the play and can take people on and size-up situations.'

That's Trevor Brooking, footballer. Off-field he likes to relax by enjoying pop music and other sports, particularly tennis.

Trevor, whose birthday falls on 2 October, is engaged to a Finnish girl he met at his brother's wedding – Tony also married a Finnish girl – and he and Hilkka Helekorpi plan a 1970 wedding. There won't be any eligible bachelors in the West Ham first-team squad when Trevor and Billy Bonds both get married next year.

Trevor has the simplest of all ambitions in soccer – 'to go on as long as possible in football'. His overall target is a full international cap - 'you've got to aim for that all the time in this game'.

Soccer for this 6ft. 1½in. product of the modern school is nearly a 12-months-a-year occupation. Trevor reported for training for last season in July 1968 and did not 'break-up' until mid-June 1969. At the end of the season he travelled to America with the West Ham first-team squad; he returned from America and went on to Italy to take part in an Under-21 tournament.

The Hammers were based at Baltimore in the American competition and played against Wolves, Dundee United, Aston Villa and Kilmarnock at 'home'! Then they travelled to Dallas, Kansas City, St. Louis and Atlanta for the return games.

The Hammers beat Dundee United 8–2 on a tartan turf surface in Portland, Oregon, and lost 1–2 to Kilmarnock on Astroturf. They also played Spurs in an exhibition match and lost 3–4.

A British official in Portland who watched the Hammers in devastating form against Dundee United on the tartan turf surface said that all the excitement was taken out of the game because the ball moved too smoothly. His suggestion that it was too easy for the Hammers playing on the surface brought the retort from manager Greenwood: 'Well, Dundee United haven't found it too easy!'

'We played well that day – the tartan turf made passing easier and it suited our style,' says Trevor. 'I found the tartan turf the better of the two surfaces. It had more of a carpety effect.'

Unfortunately, from a comparison point of view, the experiment on Astroturf was made on a narrow pitch and the midfield players found themselves cramped and with little room to work.

While in America the Hammers played the experimental rule that players could not be offside from free kicks, but Trevor felt that this innovation did not create the goalmouth incident that was expected.

West Ham came second to Wolves in the competition, which was run on the lines of six points for a win, three for a draw and one for every goal up to three. A maximum nine points per game created some additional interest.

Trevor says of the attempt to stabilise soccer in the States: 'It will be a long job. Baseball and basketball are big out there and American football is the major attraction.'

The crowds at Baltimore to see the Hammers were in the 3,500–

It's a goal. Trevor Brooking beats Eire international Jim Conway and goalkeeper Tony Macedo in the air to head a goal against Fulham at Upton Park.

It's not quite a goal. . . . Trevor Brooking dives in to head the ball and gives Southampton goalkeeper Gerry Gurr an anxious moment. Recognise the other Southampton player? It's former Hammer Joe Kirkup.

5,000 range, disappointing to the organisers although, as Trevor noted, those who did attend were as keen and excited as any he had experienced.

The Hammers stopped at Bermuda en route to London and Trevor bought some drums with him. He left them in the rack of the 'plane at London Airport and, when he went back for them, he was left behind by the team coach. Trevor arrived home in Romford – just in time to get manager Greenwood's call to go to Italy the next day. He and Jimmy Lindsay, who was due to holiday in Scotland, joined the Under-21 side.

Just to give some idea of what the Hammers of the future may look like, here is the team that represented West Ham against the cream of the young players of Inter-Milan, Torino, Lanerossi and Juventus – Steve Death; Bob Glozier, Frank Lampard; Pat Holland, Peter Keary, Keith Miller; Tim Clements, Lindsay, Brooking, Roger Cross, Dave Llewelyn.

Death, Lampard – 'he looked good, back to normal after his long injury lay-off' says Trevor – Holland, Lindsay, Brooking and Cross have all made first-team appearances. Welsh centre-half Stuart Morgan had his foot put in plaster after an injury in an early game and had to fly home; unlucky deputy Keary put through his own goal for the only score of the Final against Lanerossi.

The Hammers headed their group by beating Inter-Milan 2–0 and drawing with Torino (0–0) and Lanerossi (1–1). They beat Juventus 3–1 in the semi-final, but lost 1–0 to Lanerossi in the last match.

After an 11-months season and all that travel, where did Trevor holiday last summer? 'At home in England,' he answered with a smile.'

He is a strong advocate of the life of a professional footballer. 'I like playing and I like travelling,' he says. 'Although I am not a good sight-seer, I get to places through football that I would never reach in a lifetime otherwise.'

He lists as his most enjoyable games the two home victories in April 1968, 5–0 against Newcastle and 3–0 against Nottingham Forest. The hat-trick Trevor scored against Newcastle – the only hat-trick of his career – helped make that match memorable.

Looking at six-footer Trevor – he weighs a sizeable 12 stone 12 pounds - it is difficult to credit that he used to be apprehensive of playing alongside World Cup stars Bobby Moore, Geoff Hurst and Martin Peters.

The reason? 'They were in the side when I was still at school,' he says. 'I used to talk about them when I was a boy – then I was playing alongside them. I don't mean I had a complex, or anything like that, but it took some time for me to get used to being with them. Moore, Hurst and Peters sounded right. I wasn't sure that Brooking was in that class.

That's Trevor Brooking. Modest, yet ambitious enough to want to play alongside Bobby Moore and Co. in an England shirt. A young man who knows what he wants out of life. I reckon he is more likely to get an 'A' level than an 'O' level when they mark up his soccer career.

He is a product of an era of unrestricted wages – one of the modern breed. Yet he is also a typical product of the West Ham system. He has earned a right to be in the company of some of England's top players. One of these days a youngster will say to him: 'I remember you as a star player when I was at school.'

2

Happy to Help – that's Albert Walker

Thirty-seven years have passed since Albert Walker, a self-styled country lad from Lancashire, arrived wide-eyed at the big London railway terminus to join West Ham. He is still there.

Albert, a gentle-spoken 58-year-old who has retained more than a trace of his native accent despite his years among East Londoners, is designated team-attendant to the West Ham first team. His major function, he says, is to help the players.

'Everyone's job at Upton Park is to make the players happy,' he says. 'I like to help. The number one quality required in my position is understanding.'

The story of Albert Walker is typical of what makes the Hammers tick over nicely in their proud role of family club supreme. He is an ex-player . . . a man who has devoted a lifetime to the West Ham cause . . . a man indoctrinated with the club ideals and able to achieve results without bawling or shouting abuse. A true product of the West Ham school.

He was born at Little Lever, near Bolton, and played as an amateur for Southport before signing professional for his home-town club, Bolton Wanderers. After a season with them he moved to Barrow. The next step was to join the Hammers in the summer of 1932.

'Coming to London was an event for me – like going abroad,' he says.

I don't know the fee involved – nor does Albert – but West Ham got a bargain when former scout Ned Liddell arranged for him to move south when Barrow were unable to pay his wages.

World Cup star Martin Peters was one of the players who 'came through the ranks' with Albert Walker.

Let Albert tell the story in his own words: 'I received a telegram in the close season to travel to Barrow. Ned Liddell, who recently died at the age of 90, met me and asked if I would like to join West Ham. He offered me terms and, with Barrow owing me money, how could I refuse?'

Albert joined West Ham at a wage of £7 10s. a week, soon raised to the maximum wage of the time, £8.

When he arrived at Euston Station en route to Upton Park he had to find his own way to the ground and had difficulty in making himself understood because of his broad tones.

'How do I get to East Ham?' he asked repeatedly, and when he was finally told he had to catch a Barking train he misunderstood the

Albert Walker in action against Spurs.

Londoner trying to help him. He'd never heard of Barking – a barking train baffled him at first!

Albert moved into 'digs' near East Ham Station and met former West Ham manager, Charlie Paynter, the trainer at that time, who left a lasting impression because of the straw panama hat and the smoking jacket he wore. Albert had been used to peak caps in his football career until then.

He played nine games in the reserves at right-back, then switched to the left-flank to get into the first team. And left-back he remained. The man he replaced for his first team debut was Alf Chalkley, who returned to the side to partner him. The Walker-Chalkley combination was established.

Albert played his 100th consecutive League game at Leicester on Good Friday, 1936, a milestone he recalls with pride. 'It is every player's ambition to play 100 games and my run was eventually broken when I went down with flu. The club sent me to Southend to get over it.'

In those days when jet travel and floodlights were years in the future, a day at Southend was an accepted feature of Cup training and preparation for West Ham, who went to the sea and sampled a dozen oysters as a sort of ritual.

'There was more running without a football in our training sessions then,' Albert recalls. 'On Tuesday morning we would get a ball and, generally, at the back end of the season, we would be allowed on to the pitch with slippers on.'

Albert played with some of the finest players in West Ham history, England internationals Jimmy Ruffell, Len Goulden, Jackie Morton, Vic Watson and Big Jim Barrett.

Big Jim Barrett was the character of the time, a great player reckons Albert and, as a personality, 'larger than life'.

When Albert joined the Hammers they had just been demoted to the Second Division and struggled to avoid relegation again in his first season with the club. But they reached the semi-final of the Cup.

Everton beat the Hammers 2–1 at Wolverhampton, the winner coming in the final stages, and went on to beat Manchester City 3–0 at Wembley. Dixie Dean, a name to be reckoned with in those days, was the Everton centre-forward but, says Albert, Big Jim Barrett played him out of the game.

That semi-final ranks as the highlight, and the low point, of Albert's playing career. 'It was sad because the semi-final is the worst round to get knocked out,' he says.

West Ham were in their gay deceivers mood in those days of the

Goalkeeper Herman Conway takes the ball from the feet of Tottenham forward Morrison at Upton Park. Albert Walker is there as cover.

1930s. The first season in the Second Division proved an anti-climax, but the Hammers missed a return to the top grade by goal average one year and did reasonably well in others.

What does Albert recall of his playing contemporaries? Ruffell, who played six times for England and over 500 times for West Ham, was a big star – 'a lively player . . . if he was caught offside twice in a season that was it'.

Len Goulden was a keen student of the game when he was a player and Jackie Morton, the slim winger known as 'The Eel', was one of the best players of his time. Puddefoot, when he returned to Upton Park, was still capable of immense skill with the ball.

But, as I have said, the over-riding character was Big Jim Barrett. Albert recalls a trip to Plymouth for a last game of the season, the only time during the nine months that the Hammers had been safe from the fear of relegation. With the tension off and the realisation that Second Division football was assured for another year they went on to the field at Home Park – and were three goals down in ten minutes.

The day before the match some of the players went into a fish-and-chip shop, where Big Jim had them in an uproar when he pulled the brim of his hat down over his eyes and addressed the woman serving behind the counter: 'Fish and a pennorth for little Jimmy.'

One of Albert's recollections of the time is of Big Jim returning for training each season at his end-of-summer weight of around 17 stone. The photographers loved Big Jim; invariably there was a shot of him encased in a couple of thick roll-neck sweaters holding a comparative lightweight playing colleague in either hand.

Albert returned North in 1938 to play for Doncaster Rovers and after the war he returned South again to join Colchester United and link up with former West Ham wing-half Ted Fenton, who was to succeed Charlie Paynter as manager. Ted eventually asked Albert to join the Upton Park staff and he rejoined the Hammers in 1949.

The late Billy Moore was the trainer at the time and Albert who, in turn, looked after the Metropolitan League and reserve sides, eventually succeeded this former star West Ham player.

'I came up through the ranks,' he says with pride.

In his days as a player Albert became geared to the West Ham way of life. He remembers a player being sent upstairs at an hotel in Preston for not wearing a jacket. Charlie Paynter, the father figure to all Hammers of several decades, used to put his arm round a player's shoulder – 'you felt better for it', says Albert.

One player who shall remain nameless was finished at Upton Park because of a foul he committed in a game.

'Charlie Paynter still asks me about my family to this day,' says Albert.

He rates Joe Cockroft, who joined West Ham from Gainsborough Trinity and was in the first team after a couple of weeks, one of the best uncapped players of his time.

Big Jim was always in the middle, as steady as a rock, and on the other flank there was Jim Collins and then Ted Fenton. Bob Dixon was the goalkeeper when Albert arrived at Upton Park.

There were no youth teams as there are nowadays, but boys joined the groundstaff. More players graduated from the Midland or Southern Leagues because development was later – West Ham did well out of Gainsborough Trinity, for example with the signing of Jackie Morton, Cockroft and goalkeeper Herman Conway.

GRADUATES

A young centre-forward named Noel Cantwell was sent to play for Albert Walker when he had charge of the 'B' team at Upton Park. And the well-built young Irishman arrived for his first game minus any football boots. Five minutes before the kick-off, Albert recalls, he had to rush to the Dagenham ground to borrow a selection of boots so that Cantwell could make his debut.

Cantwell, now manager of Coventry, won 17 Eire international caps as a full-back; his tuition for League football came under Albert Walker's astute guidance in the West Ham 'B' team.

John Bond was another graduate of the side, making his debut in a park at Dagenham. Bond and Cantwell were later to develop as one of the finest full-back partnerships in West Ham history.

Harry Hooper, the flying winger who became an England 'B' international, was with Albert Walker's 'A' team; so was Ken Brown, a worthy centre-half successor to Big Jim Barrett and Dick Walker, and an England international in 1959.

Albert Walker saw Ken playing in a junior match and reported on his prowess to Ted Fenton. Ken played for a side in the same League and switched to West Ham where he made 386 league appearances.

Bobby Moore, Geoff Hurst and Martin Peters are three of the moderns who have graduated from Albert Walker's sides in the lower ranks. John Smith, a Swindon star in the 1969 Football League Cup Final defeat of Arsenal at Wembley, was a groundstaff boy who played in the reserves at the age of 16.

West Ham's semi-final defeat of Manchester United in 1964 was Albert's happiest memory as a watcher of football rather than a player. 'The atmosphere was electric and everyone in the West Ham camp was keyed up to do well. It was most thrilling,' he says.

Before the game Albert left the dressing room at Hillsborough, Sheffield, and found two of the Manchester United team chatting to some of the Dagenham Girl Pipers who played at the match.

'I went back and saw the atmosphere in our dressing room and I knew we were going to win,' says Albert.

He praises West Ham as a progressive club which always considers the comfort of spectators; he acknowledges his allegiance by his devotion to successive generations of players of all ages.

'You get to know their mannerisms on match days,' he says. 'You develop a feeling of how they are going to play. It's a West Ham atmosphere. When players leave Upton Park they are sorry. They

A Royal occasion. Prince Charles of Sweden, shielding 'Big Jim' Barrett, meets Albert Walker before a pre-war match. The other West Ham players (*from left to right*) are: goalkeeper Herman Conway, Jackie Morton, Alf Chalkley, Jim Collins, Len Goulden, Ted Fenton, Dr. Marshall and Joe Cockroft.

keep coming back to visit us – it's something here, not something that has been built up over twelve months. It's . . . West Ham.'

The words speak volumes for Albert Walker, whose relaxations away from soccer are gardening and fishing. He won't hear a word against his club. He won't get involved in controversy of comparing various eras. He is happy to be around 37 years later. Happy to help . . . the West Ham club and the West Ham players.

3

Ernie Gregory – an all-time great who gave 90 minutes

When young Ernie Gregory joined West Ham as a boy the late chairman, Mr. W. J. Cearns, said to him: 'If you do it for 90 minutes every Saturday you can stay here for life.'

Ernie is still around Upton Park 33 years later, 21 of them as a player, so he must have done his stuff quite well!

When I was a youngster watching professional football the goal-keepers were giants of men . . . Frank Swift . . . Sam Bartram . . . and Ernie Gregory. Great goalies, great characters. It was a long time before I could get used to the idea of anyone but Ernie Gregory minding the West Ham net when his illustrious playing career came to a close.

Ernie is 47 now and a coach at Upton Park. A respected figure on the West Ham scene – and in the Hammers' folklore of recent decades. He is an imposing figure of 6ft. 1in. and, although I wouldn't guarantee his weight is still at his favourite level for football (13 stone 10 pounds), he is a fit man.

He is, without repeating myself too much, a typical West Ham product. Reared in the game by former manager Charlie Paynter, his loyalty to the club has been unswerving from the day he signed as a wide-eyed 14-year-old back in April 1936.

Ernie was never booked in his long playing career and never entertained serious thought of leaving Upton Park although clubs such as Arsenal and Manchester United had him on their wanted list.

He was born down the road at Stratford and came into West Ham's orbit when Charlie Paynter saw him playing for the district schoolboy side. He was a big youngster, around 5ft. 11in. when he played for

Ernie Gregory – more than 30 years at Upton Park.

England Schoolboys against the Rest of England, and as keenly interested in cricket and swimming as in football.

The odd fact is that he never played in goal for his school side, St. Paul's at Stratford. He fancied himself as a defender. He only went in goal because his brother, Bob, broke a leg playing soccer and Ernie, as a Gregory and a big fellow, seemed the obvious deputy.

'I went in goal,' says Ernie. 'But I never liked it. I was much happier playing out.'

He slotted in well enough, though, to be chosen for West Ham schoolboys and for Essex and London representative sides. Eventually Charlie Paynter, watching the district side to check on the local talent, saw the possibilities of young Ernie.

Charlie Paynter put his arm round the youngster's shoulder and asked: 'How would you like to stay with Uncle Charlie?' It was his way of inviting Ernie to join the West Ham groundstaff.

'Come and see my Ma,' replied Ernie, whose father had died when he was ten.

The day Charlie Paynter arrived outside the Gregory house to sign young Ernie on amateur forms he drove a green Hillman. The kids of the neighbourhood clustered around in admiration – a car was an object of admiration in Stratford in the mid-1930s. There were few of them about.

When Mrs. Gregory agreed to young Ernie fulfilling his ambition and joining the Hammers, Charlie Paynter told her: 'He has got to wear a collar and tie.'

'I wanted to be a footballer and I thought that Charlie was West Ham,' recalls Ernie.

Other clubs were wooing young Ernie to join them but, although he was not strictly a West Ham supporter – 'I always wanted to play, not watch' – he had no hesitation in throwing in his lot with Charlie Paynter.

Over three decades later he still talks with the same admiration of the former West Ham manager, who offered him £1 a week to join the groundstaff.

Charlie Paynter told him: 'Give your Ma fifteen shillings. Keep five for yourself.'

Ernie obeyed – and began his soccer apprenticeship by weeding the Upton Park pitch and doing such chores as sweeping out the dressing rooms.

When he was signed as a professional in 1939, he was handed a £10 signing-on fee. Charlie Paynter advised: 'Treat your mother. Put the rest in the Post Office.'

Ernie Gregory saves at the feet of Fulham's Jimmy Hill during an F.A. Cup match at Upton Park in February 1958.

Ernie did. 'His word was law to me. He was the smartest manager in the game.'

Dave Bailey, a former West Ham goalkeeper who had become a painter on the Upton Park staff, was one of the first big influences on up and coming Ernie Gregory. Bailey took Ernie to the training space in front of the ground each dinner hour and spent time improving his work in stopping shots on the ground. 'I was O.K. in the air, not so hot down below at the time because of my height,' says Ernie.

Dave Bailey's devotion to the chore made Ernie as good 'on the deck' as he was in the air, and the youngster also received help from first teamer Herman Conway, who understudied Ted Hufton, to many the Daddy of all West Ham goalkeepers.

Charlie Paynter always used to swear by Hufton as the best Hammers keeper in his half century with the club, but he eventually conceded that Ernie was the equal of the former idol.

'There were some great people around in those days – they tried to help me get on,' says Ernie.

His last game as a schoolboy was for West Ham against Preston in the English Schools' Trophy Final, a 0–0 draw at Upton Park. His first game for West Ham, at the tender age of 14, was for the reserve side against the first team in a pre-season practice before the start of the 1936–7 season.

Let Ernie reminisce in his own words. 'The great Jimmy Ruffell burst through our defence and came towards me. I remember it as if it were yesterday. The great man looked at me as if to say 'poor little so-and-so' and obviously took pity on me.

'Do you know . . . he took the ball back. Ruffell was known for his shooting power, but he went back and the outcome was that I tipped his shot over. I will never forget the gesture.'

Herman Conway and Vivian Blore were the goalkeepers at the time, and an injury in training to the latter gave Ernie his chance to shine with the stars in that public practice.

'I was shaking like a leaf,' recalls Ernie.

There were no youth systems as we know them today when Ernie Gregory was putting his first feet on the professional ladder, so he, Cater, Wood and Lewis were loaned to Leytonstone, then as now a force in the Isthmian League.

Ernie, who had previously been loaned to the Grafton Club, made his debut for Leytonstone as a 15 year old and was in the side that won the Isthmian League championship a year later. Leytonstone also reached the semi-finals of the Amateur Cup.

Ernie won several honours in amateur football – 'it was a good standard in those days' – and stayed until he was seventeen. His last game was another Amateur Cup semi-final against Bishop Auckland at Darlington, and he was injured.

In midweek Ernie played for the West Ham 'A' side, whose trainer was another present-day colleague, Wally St. Pier, now the club's chief representative.

'I didn't fancy turning professional at one stage,' admits Ernie. 'I was playing top amateur football and, when I received the Golden Jersey for my performance playing for an F.A. side against the Royal Marines, it looked a distinct possibility that I would get an England cap.'

There were five goalkeepers at West Ham in those pre-war days, Conway, Harry Medhurst, Jack Weare, George Taylor and Ernie. But he did sign as a professional in 1939, and made his debut for the first team soon after the start of the war. Harry Medhurst (now the Chelsea trainer) and Ernie took it in turns in goal in alternative matches.

'What a wonderful opportunity,' he says. 'I was playing against the likes of Ted Drake, Alf Kirchen, Jock Dodds, Jimmy Hagan, Joe Mercer, Ken Willingham and Stan Cullis, the best centre-half I ever saw.'

Great names. Great experience for Ernie. It stood him in good stead after the war. In 1946 Harry Medhurst resumed as first choice. He was replaced by George Taylor. Then Ernie took over. He was on top money for 15 years . . . and a top name goalkeeper. Injury may have ruled him out, but that was all. Ernie was a fixture.

Although he did not make his first 'official' League appearance until 1946 – his first team appearances were confined to wartime during Army service – he totalled 383 appearances, a record for a Hammers' keeper.

Today Ernie still acknowledges his debt to Charlie Paynter – 'a wonderful influence on me and a great manager. He was to us what Sir Matt Busby is to Manchester United players.'

At one stage in his career Ernie was on top form. 'If I'd turned my back the ball would have hit it,' is how he describes being 'on song'. Then, in a match against Swansea, he dropped the ball and began a bad patch that lasted some three games. Head down, he went to see Charlie Paynter to find out what had gone wrong with his form.

'He put me right – he had the ability to talk to players the right way,' says Ernie.

The name 'Gregory' only appeared on a reserve team sheet 64

times in Ernie's 21 years as a player. The rest of his games were with the stars . . . as a star.

Against Manchester City in 1949–50 he fractured a small finger when an opponent went across his hand as Ernie was taking the ball. He became despondent. A Leicester goalkeeper of the time had a similar injury and lost his finger. It was touch and go for Ernie too.

Ernie became the first West Ham player to go to London Hospital to see Mr. W. Alexander Law (still the honorary consultant today) and, although the injury kept him out of action for two months and during the summer break, he was cured.

'I felt out of the picture at the start of the next season,' says Ernie, 'but Charlie Paynter must have sensed this because he came across in training one day and told me "Get in goal for the first team". That completed the cure.'

The removal of a bone from a wrist following an injury against Blackpool in a Cup-tie meant Ernie missing nearly the whole of a season. In his time he collected a few of the injuries that are a goal-keeper's stock-in-trade, nose, head and groin.

'I don't go with this hooey that goalkeepers are touched,' says Ernie. 'They joke about it – you don't have to be mad to be a goalie, but it helps! I can't agree. A goalkeeper has to be courageous and I believe that if you haven't got a good goalkeeper you haven't got a side. A goalkeeper doing his job correctly makes a defence.'

Ernie has always been a student of goalkeeping and, as a coach, he contends that a goalie sees all that is happening on the field and is able to study and know his own side's weaknesses. A goalkeeper studies his defence and helps out when he can.

One day an Eire selector arrived at Upton Park to study Noel Cantwell, the former West Ham left-back who is now managing Coventry City.

'I knew the selector was there and I spoke Noel through the game,' he recalls.

Reading the play and observing the strengths and weaknesses of individuals and tactics are part and parcel of the job of a coach. Ernie contends they are part of the make-up of a goalkeeper.

'I used to think about a game endlessly after the final whistle,' he says. 'I was somewhat unflappable as a player. Now I am a coach sometimes it comes out when I watch . . . my emotions bubble over. I still play now, you know. I sit in the stand and play more or less every ball that is played.'

Ernie Gregory teaches his goalkeepers – they are all 'my goalkeepers' when you discuss them with him – to make a cup as they catch a ball

Ernie Gregory watches apprehensively as a shot from Blackburn Rovers inside-left Bill Smith (*left*) shaves the outside of the post in an F.A. Cup fifth round replay at Blackburn in February 1956.

and to use their legs and knees in making saves. 'You can see my goalkeepers from the way I train them,' he says.

The highlight of Ernie's career was being a regular member of the side that took West Ham to promotion from the Second Division in season 1957–8 and ended a run of 26 years in the lower class. I well remember Ernie as saviour of the side in several matches in the nine months' battle to rejoin soccer's elite.

'It was the first time we had really achieved anything in my time at Upton Park,' says Ernie, who earned recognition for the England 'B' side but did not win a full international cap because he belonged to an era of great goalkeepers. Maybe the Hammers, as a Second Division outfit, were unfashionable at the time.

Ernie WAS disappointed at missing selection for England and many experts regarded him as a natural successor in the international team to the late, great Frank Swift. I would have thought he was ready made for a cap – but the likes of Ted Ditchburn, Bert Williams, Gil Merrick, George Swindin, Bernard Streten and Sam Bartram had their advocates.

'There were loads of good goalkeepers – all of them personalities,' says Ernie. 'You don't get the same personality now.'

More's the pity. As one who was brought up to believe that a good goalkeeper was a big, commanding figure of a man, I am sorry to record the departure of the happy breed.

Ernie Gregory rates England's Gordon Banks as one from the old school, and nominates Chelsea's Peter Bonetti, who has also won recent international calls, as the current tops in this country. 'Bonetti,' he says, 'is willing to come all the way to take a ball' – and that's how Ernie likes it for a keeper.

'I don't believe in centre-halves clearing from under the goal-keeper's nose,' he says. 'The keeper must be the guv'nor. That's a good definition – he must command his area.'

Ted Hufton, Ernie's greatest rival in the goalkeeping affections of long-time Upton Park regulars, gave his successor many good tips – and Ernie has passed on his knowledge to those that have come after him. When Ernie was 38 the Hammers bought Noel Dwyer from Wolves as a probable replacement and, although he had the potential of greatness, he never established himself.

Ernie acknowledges the influence on him of playing behind Big Jim Barrett in the reserves, and also speaks admiringly of his close friend, Dick Walker, Barrett's eventual successor and the longest serving West Ham player. He was around for 24 years, three more than Ernie.

I asked Ernie to nominate his best-ever Hammers team since the 1930s, but he hedged slightly and said: 'There were three good teams.'

The first: the team that set out on the 1939–40 season with high hopes of promotion. The war intervened.

The second: Ernie's own promotion-winning side of 1957-8.

And, thirdly: the present-day side. 'I wouldn't put them in any order or compare one against the other,' says Ernie.

He is a staunch believer that West Ham would have been in the First Division in 1940 if Herr Hitler had not thrown a spanner into football's bolts. 'There was such ability in that side,' he recalls. 'The club had bought two players to help clinch promotion and we had a hell of a lot of good youngsters coming up. Charlie Paynter believed in getting kids to back the seniors.'

Coach at Upton Park just before the war was Bob John, the Wales and Arsenal wing-half, and Ernie pays tribute to him as yet another influence on his development because of John's training ideas.

This was what Ernie calls 'a good side – a very good side': Harry Medhurst; Charlie Bicknell, Charlie Walker; Norman Corbett or Ted Fenton, Dick Walker, Joe Cockroft; Stan Foxall or 'Dizzy' Burton (signed from Wolves), Archie MacAulay, Sammy Small or Cliff Hubbard (signed from Hull), Len Goulden, Jackie Morton.

Then, of course, there was Ernie's own team: Gregory; John Bond, Noel Cantwell; Andy Malcolm, Ken Brown (succeeding Malcolm Allison), Bill Lansdowne or Andy Nelson; Mike Grice, John Smith, Vic Keeble, John Dick, Malcolm Musgrove.

Ernie won't say it, but I will. Len Goulden would be the first choice of both of us for a select side from the pre-war teams and those of the 1957–8 and present eras – you take your choice with the rest.

In Ernie's days as a top-flight goalkeeper the opposition boasted players of the calibre of Tom Lawton, who could climb for a ball as high as any keeper, but the one centre-forward Ernie dreaded meeting was Ted Drake, of Arsenal.

'He'd take you and the ball into the back of the net,' he recalls.

The hardest shot he ever encountered belonged to an unknown with Manchester City, but Ernie remembers with grudging admiration (grudging because he was a goalkeeper) the terrific drive of Frank Neary and the shooting of Jimmy Hagan – 'a great player, but he could let it go, too'.

The greatest goalkeeper of Ernie's time, he says, was Frank Swift, but he has a lot of respect for the Russian Lev Yashin.

It is a tribute to Ernie's reputation that Bobby Ferguson, although a world record fee goalkeeper, still spends hours accepting advice on their art. Ernie spends extra time with *his* goalkeepers, from Ferguson to the humblest young amateur.

There was more character in the game in Ernie's day. He grew up with two of the greatest dressing room influences, Big Jim Barrett and Dick Walker, and recalls: 'Even Charlie Paynter could give a tap dance as well as anyone.

'But if you got a rollicking from Charlie you knew you deserved one.'

The Fenton and Corbett brothers played together at West Ham and helped the family club image. Big Jim Barrett was succeeded by his son, Jim, now coaching Queen's Park Rangers.

'It's a wonderful atmosphere at Upton Park,' says Ernie. 'West Ham was the only club I wanted to play for. Others wanted me, but I would never have left.'

Arsenal were one club that wanted Ernie, who guested for Q.P.R. during the war, and they sent inside-forward Alex James, he of the long, baggy shorts, to run the rule over him. 'I had it off that day,' says Ernie, his description of a good game.

Although there was nothing official about a bid a West Ham director of the time was heard to say: 'Arsenal haven't enough money to buy Ernie.'

Football in Ernie's day was played off the cuff. He learned the tricks of the Tommy Lawtons, the Eddie Quigleys ('he tried to send you the other way by using his shoulders') and the Peter Dohertys.

Ernie rated Doherty a 'fantastic player', who had the ability to change feet for a shot as he moved at speed. 'I still say to my boys

Charlie Paynter had a wonderful influence on Ernie Gregory. 'He was to us what Sir Matt Busby is to Manchester United players,' says Gregory.

Albert Walker (*left*) and Ernie Gregory relax during a break from pre-season training.

"Watch the ball and nothing else. Peter proved it's no good watching their feet. Goalkeepers have to get this sort of knowledge." '

Ernie was kicked on the head four times early in his career. He thought about how to avoid this – and came up with the idea of spreading himself and using his feet too when he dived at the feet of an advancing forward.

There's less thought now than then. 'Goalies today let their defenders do a fair proportion of their work,' says Ernie.

The Hammers awarded Ernie benefits and a testimonial when he finished playing. He also received the Football League's official long-service statuette.

Some small measure of appreciation to one of the biggest-hearted players ever to turn out for the Hammers. Today he is a fully qualified coach who has benefited from the experience of another mentor – present manager Ron Greenwood.

Ernie had Martin Peters under his charge as an 'A' team player and remembers the satisfaction he got from seeing a world-class player in the making – a compensation to this West Ham-minded fanatic when his playing days ended.

The Gregory garden gets attention from Ernie when he wants to relax, but he admits: 'Football is my hobby.'

Ernie comes from a pre-war era when West Ham players had to look after their own playing gear and when Charlie Paynter insisted on creases down the centre of the shorts.

Ernie never missed a train to an away game. He never missed a training session.

He was brought up to believe that a goalkeeper, the centre-half and the centre-forward were the backbone of a side – the others were 'targets'.

He was brought up to believe that football was a simple game played off the cuff.

That's why Ernie delights in saying: 'Some of the old stuff is coming back as we reach the end of the 1960s. It's new to the kids of today . . . but it is the old stuff.'

Ernie, I am pleased to acknowledge, was of the right stuff himself. A personality goalkeeper. A one-club devotee. Good enough to be compared on equal terms with Frank Swift. He certainly gave West Ham 90 minutes of effort in return for his wages.

Thirty-three years a Hammer . . . and still going strong.

4

West Ham Players have too much respect, says Billy Bonds

If you need convincing that success is going to cap the efforts of a side that has a reputation of being the most entertaining in the country on its day then I suggest you absorb the words of Billy Bonds.

The 22-year-old England Under-23 right-back – I think that's his basic position, although he has played in a few in his time at Upton Park – told me during last summer: 'Next year West Ham could really do something – if we keep tightening up.

'We slackened off a bit towards the end of the 1968–69 season, but next year . . . IT COULD BE OUR SEASON.'

That's fighting talk from a self-confessed easy-going character, who has made himself a popular figure around the Upton Park scene since he arrived from Charlton in exchange for a fee of £47,500 in May 1967. Last season he was second to Geoff Hurst in the 'Hammer of the Year' poll.

Billy – West Ham will have to pay more to Charlton if he wins an England cap in the future – is an adventurous, modern full-back. He is big (6 ft. 1 in. tall), strong (12 stone 10 pounds) and fast. Manager Ron Greenwood calls him 'a great competitor'.

The transfer cost the Hammers comparatively little. Billy succeeded Joe Kirkup when he was sold to Chelsea for £35,000 and Dennis Burnett, transferred to Millwall for £15,000. With the emergence of Frank Lampard, Bobby Howe and John Charles, who cost nothing, the Hammers got a bargain full-back partnership.

Billy was born at Woolwich in 1946 and played for the local

Billy Bonds is a great favourite with the West Ham crowd.

schoolboy district side before being chosen to captain Kent. Jock Basford, the former Charlton coach who is now with Mansfield, saw him playing in the county side and he went to The Valley as a Charlton youngster at the age of 13. He had trials for England Youth.

He took a job as an apprentice in a factory for six months when he left school – 'but I got fed up with that'.

Charlton decided to sign him as an apprentice professional footballer when he was 15 and he made his way through the ranks of the South East Counties and the Metropolitan Leagues to the reserves.

Billy made his League début for Charlton against Northampton at the age of 18, a tough task as Northampton were then at the top of the table and Charlton needed the points to win and escape relegation. The result: a satisfying 1–1 draw, although Billy recalls Northampton as a 'very physical side'.

He succeeded Scottish international John Hewie, the South African-born full-back, at The Valley and was an ever-present in the Charlton side in the Second Division in 1966–67.

Billy, who has a brother and a sister, finally aroused the interest of the big clubs and, in his own words, 'there were a couple of them in for me, but Bob Stokoe, the Charlton manager at the time, wanted me to go to West Ham'.

That posed no problems. Ron Greenwood signed Billy after watching him in a game against Birmingham, and then Billy watched the Hammers draw 1–1 with Manchester City before his début.

Billy says: 'Bob Stokoe was a great bloke. I started getting the write-ups at Charlton as we struggled against relegation, and I knew there were several First Division clubs after me.

'I thought I would have to go to Sunderland or Leicester, or somewhere, which I wasn't keen to do because I was born in Woolwich and have always lived south of the river in London.

'One day Mr. Stokoe said "I've got a club for you and I'd like you to sign for them, but it's up to you."

'I was amazed and delighted when I heard it was West Ham. I had not thought of them and, of course, I was only too glad to join.'

Billy's first impression of West Ham was that the side gave away goals too easily. The Hammers lost 3–2 to Sheffield Wednesday on his début . . . but he reckons that problem of soft goals has been conquered now.

Billy has won two England Under-23 caps and has been a regular in the West Ham side. Signing for the Hammers thrilled him 'to bits' as he knew the reputation of the side and the club, but he was equally pleased that he did not have to pick up roots as his new soccer home was just the other side of the River Thames, a half-hour journey.

The personalities in the West Ham side impressed, but did not overawe, the young recruit from the Second Division. 'Playing at West Ham has helped my skills,' he says. 'Ron Greenwood's main objective is the skills of the game and, although we do our share of running, the emphasis in training is on skill.

'Playing with such good players has helped me tremendously. It's an education playing with Bobby Moore, for example. He gets away with things no ordinary footballer could pull off. Often he looks to have lost the ball, but somehow he gets it away. He is a big man, but he seems able to squeeze past people. The sort of situation where I would be grateful just to kick it away . . . Bobby's there putting the ball right on Geoff Hurst's chest.

'Geoff, of course, is the greatest as a striker. He is always finding space, always making himself a target for you to find. Then there's Martin Peters. He has this habit of nipping in and scoring goals that don't look at all "on".

'But they're all good players. John Charles has come on and has played well. It's strange to recall that I didn't think West Ham would want me because they seemed to have plenty of full backs.'

Billy is fond of overlapping and adding his weight to the attack with his sorties. In fact, he has played as a forward on several occasions. Ron Greenwood has played Billy in five different shirts – 2, 3, 4, 7 and 8.

The sight of Billy, hair flowing and determination on his face, has endeared him to the Upton Park regulars. They love his attacking bent. 'The crowd was good to me from the first couple of games,' he recalls. 'That's important to a player. They seemed to be on my side and that helped me settle.'

Life in the First Division with West Ham has opened new doors to Billy Bonds. He enjoys playing at Old Trafford and Anfield – 'great places to play' – but retains a soft spot for Portman Road, Ipswich, as he always seems to be on the winning side there and the pitch is one of the best in the country.

He says: 'Upton Park is a good ground, too. So are the crowd. They have a tradition at West Ham for wanting to be entertained. I certainly think we entertain them.'

Billy rates England international Bobby Charlton as the greatest player in the game today, and nominates last season's F.A. Cup defeat at Mansfield as his biggest playing disappointment. His major

Bonds duels with David Connor, the Manchester City utility man, at Upton Park.

ambition, like that of so many at Upton Park, is to see the club win the League title.

'I always seem to notch a goal a season,' Billy reminded me. I saw his fine effort in the 5–2 defeat of Coventry at Upton Park last March; the previous season he 'notched' against Spurs.

Self-analysis is not easy for a player. I asked Billy to tell me his major asset and his simple answer was: 'I like to think I play for the team.'

He is full of praise for the influence of his family on his career, and also heaps praise on Jock Basford, the coach who discovered him and who, ironically, was the Mansfield coach that dark night when the Hammers were ousted from the Cup by the Third Division outfit.

'Jock told me afterwards that their tactics were to throw the long ball into our penalty area as they felt we were not clearing quickly enough,' says Billy.

Gardening and a 'bit of golf' are the hobbies of this gentle giant, who enjoys a game of rummy on away trips with skipper Moore, Harry Redknapp and Trevor Brooking.

Do nice guys win anything in the hard, professional world of soccer ? Billy is interesting on the question and I record his views as a recent arrival at Upton Park who is in process of indoctrination to the West Ham way of life.

He says: 'There isn't anyone around to get a hold of us. That's what we need. There is not enough talking on the field. I talk . . . so does Alan Stephenson.

'BUT EVERYONE AT WEST HAM HAS TOO MUCH RESPECT. THEY THINK EVERYONE IS CAPABLE OF DOING A JOB.

'A character in the side might help us. Bobby Moore does his bit by example to inspire and lead us. I respect people, but I'm not frightened of them. Reputations don't bother me. The West Ham lads are a nice bunch of boys to get on with.'

Too nice ? I wonder. It's certainly an interesting point that they have such respect for each other's capabilities that they don't shout and call at each other as much as they might.

There is much in football today that passes as professionalism but is better described in less complimentary terms. Billy talks of teams playing 'dirty hard'.

He says: 'There is a lot of dirty play in the game today. It's "in" you might say, and there are several teams who have players who chop down the opposition. Everyone in the game knows who they are, the player who will go over the top of the ball if they think it necessary to stop an opponent.

It's a hair-raising moment when Billy Bonds meets Liverpool's £100,000 Alun Evans in an aerial duel.

On your mark, get set . . . Billy Bonds in action against Liverpool.

'This is one thing which is absolutely out at West Ham. Ron Greenwood is dead set against us chopping anyone. He expects us to go in for the ball, but never to hurt, or try to hurt, an opponent.'

When Billy arrived at Upton Park from Charlton he was surprised to hear Ron Greenwood say 'Call me Ron'.

Billy had called his previous managers 'Boss' as a mark of respect, yet here was a man for whom he had tremendous respect asking him to be familiar.

'But that's the way it is at West Ham. It's a great club, and not merely out on the field. I think it all stems from Ron. He's such a nice fellow. They say you can't be a nice guy and a success in football management, but he proves that theory wrong.'

Billy disputes that West Ham sacrifice defence for attack. He says: 'We are much tighter than we used to be. What people don't realise is that 10 players on the field are encouraged to go forward in attack when it is on, all except goalkeeper Bobby Ferguson, of course. This sometimes leaves gaps, but it's good to watch.'

You can say that again. Billy Bonds was bought to help stiffen the West Ham defence. The goals against figures prove he has played his part in that direction, but he has added weight to attack as well.

'I couldn't be happier playing for West Ham,' says Billy. A sentiment echoed, I am sure, by hordes of Hammers' supporters. They couldn't be happier that he is playing for the Hammers.

5

Rob Jenkins – Diagnosis on the Spot

The Grand National was being run at Aintree when West Ham physiotherapist Rob Jenkins hurried on to the pitch to tend an injured player.

The home inside-forward – an international of some repute – watched Jenkins at work on his charge. Then he approached the Hammers' physiotherapist and said in a quiet voice: 'I'm going to kick him again in a few minutes. Bring on the result of the Grand National next time will you?'

Rob Jenkins – full name Robert – is one of the new breed of qualified physiotherapists who have replaced the old bucket and sponge men of days not so long ago.

In typical West Ham fashion he was appointed to replace his father, the late Bill Jenkins, and provide another example of the Hammers' family club tradition.

Rob, now 31, followed in father's footsteps along the way to the First Division. Bill Jenkins joined the Hammers when Billy Moore retired in 1960; Rob succeeded his Dad as physiotherapist to Isthmian League amateurs, Walthamstow Avenue, when he qualified.

Bill Jenkins died just before the start of the 1966–7 season and his son, who had joined the Hammers to help with the youngsters and reserves, took over the first team post.

Father and son had joked about getting to the top of their chosen profession – and both regarded Wembley as the Mecca for sportsmen. Bill Jenkins was with Walthamstow Avenue when they twice reached the semi-final of the F.A. Amateur Cup; the season he joined West Ham, Avenue got to Wembley and Rob went with them.

'Mind you, Dad got there twice with the Hammers after that,' says Rob.

Bill Jenkins was one of soccer's characters and countless tales abound of the happy days in the dressing rooms at Upton Park in his reign in the first half of the 1960s.

He was born in the Rhondda, at Tylerstown, which was Jimmy Wilde country. In his young days Bill Jenkins used to win most of the mountain races in the Rhondda and was, according to his son, a 'wonderful athlete'.

'Bomber' Jenkins – that was Bill's nickname – was destined for the pits and, in fact, worked underground for a time. He was one of a family of 12 and decided that there was a better life away from his native Wales – so he joined the Army.

'He thought that was the only way out,' says Rob. 'He was a self-made man and rose to the rank of Captain in the Royal Army Medical Corps.'

That was where Rob came on the scene. Bill Jenkins served for 16 years in the Army and Rob was born at Aldershot and spent the first six years of his life in Egypt and South Africa.

During his Army days Bill Jenkins qualified as a physiotherapist and a pharmacist – and the first soccer club he became associated with when he left the Service was Clapton. Norman Corbett, the former West Ham wing-half, was in charge of the Isthmian League club then.

When Bill Jenkins moved on to Walthamstow Avenue, Rob, who was still at college, looked after Clapton. Rob was due to be a dentist, but he flunked an 'A' level and decided to follow his father into physiotherapy.

It is a far cry from the days when the magic sponge cured all ills on a soccer field. Bill Jenkins was one of the first qualified physiotherapists to arrive on the soccer scene. It took Rob three years at college to pass his exams. That's a bit different from the six weeks' course when the sponge reigned supreme.

Rob – he was the youngest qualified physiotherapist ever to get to Wembley with a team – says: 'A sponge is today the least important part of the equipment we use.'

Keeping Bobby Moore and Co. fighting fit is a responsibility that West Ham do not shirk. The club has provided equipment worth several hundreds of pounds for their dressing rooms and the annual medical bill shows that nothing is left to chance.

'I wish my wages were in the region of the medical bill,' jokes Rob Jenkins.

The healing fingers of Bill Jenkins at work on Johnny 'Budgie' Byrne.

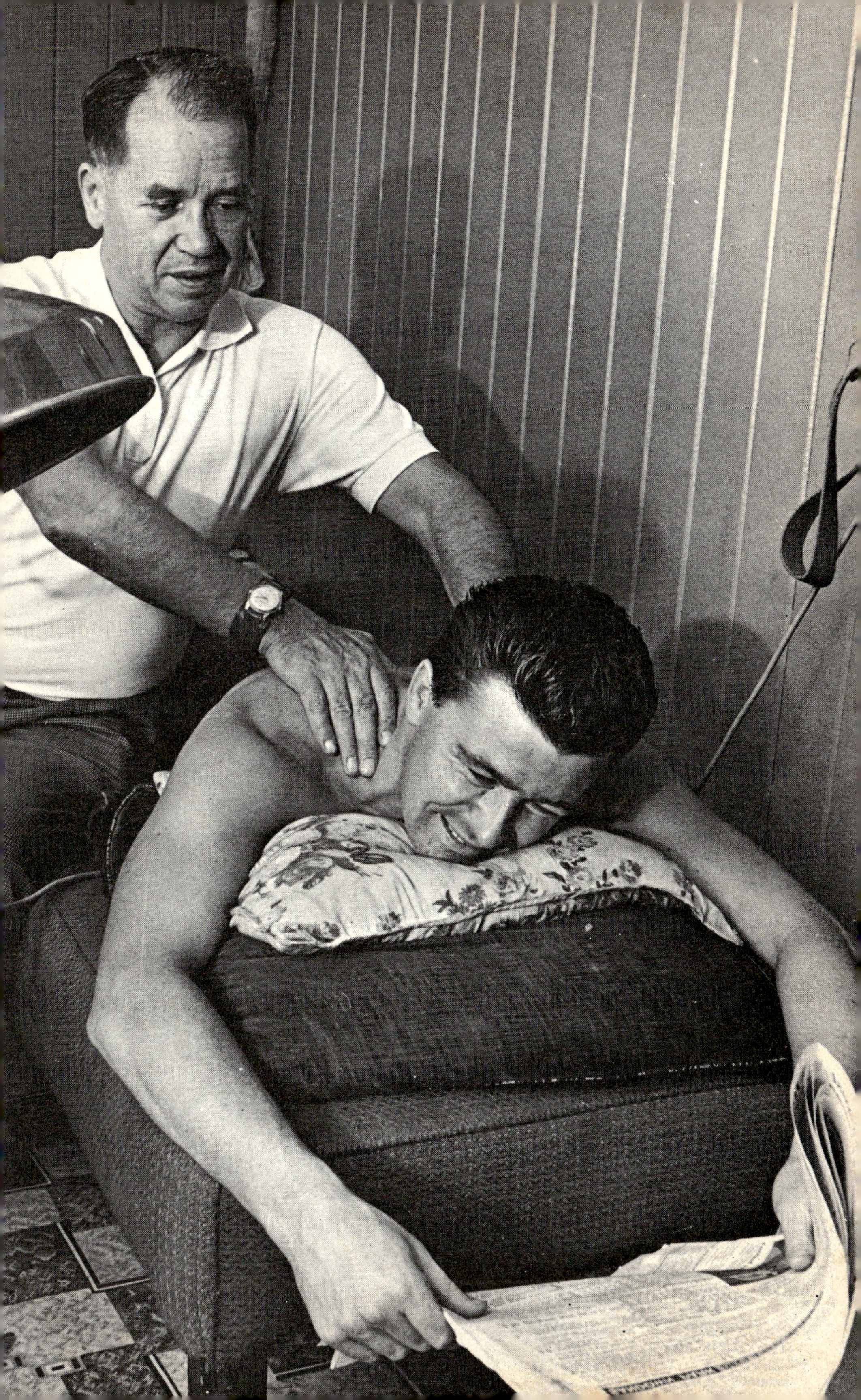

Rob sits on the line at all West Ham first team matches. He is a specialist at his job and can sum up the extent of an injury in minutes. That's why he sits at pitch level, so that he can see what has happened to a player in the way of injury and can have an idea of the damage even before he runs on to the pitch.

When substitutes were first introduced Rob had to provide a medical note saying why a player had come off the pitch; now soccer is a 12-man game it is his decision whether an injury is serious enough to necessitate one of the chosen eleven coming off in favour of the substitute.

'I can generally sum it up on the spot, whether a player is likely to be kept out for a month if we leave him on or only a week if we take him off,' says Rob.

In Bill Jenkins' day there was no alternative in the heat of a competitive match but to try and keep all eleven players on the field, even if one was injured.

Rob Jenkins is often called on for a snap decision in front of thousands of people and he does his job quickly and efficiently. His pet hate is the referee who tries to hustle him and get on with the game.

'I need time for as good a diagnosis as possible,' he says. There have been instances of players with broken legs being dragged off the field so that a referee can re-start a match without undue delay. Rob concedes he has to be quick, but he still needs time to go through one or two patterns to establish the nature of some injuries.

In some clubs the physiotherapist is used as part of the general theme of gamesmanship. A player goes down unhurt and the physiotherapist issues messages to the team to calm down or slow the game.

Not at West Ham. 'I am not a message man,' said Rob. 'The extent of any extra conversation on the field extends to wondering what horse has won a big race – never on tactics. I don't pass messages. It has never arisen at West Ham.'

Rob Jenkins might use a sponge when a player has an injured ankle, to put water inside the boot while he checks there is nothing serious amiss, but his general touchline equipment is more varied. He has a bottle of spirit, a cold spray for muscle injuries and sterilised pads of cotton-wool and lint. A physiotherapist never sponges an eye wound.

Some players these days tend to play-act and injuries are often not nearly as bad as they appear initially. That's why Rob always carries a tube of cream or a capsule of ammonia – 'a sniffer often does the trick'.

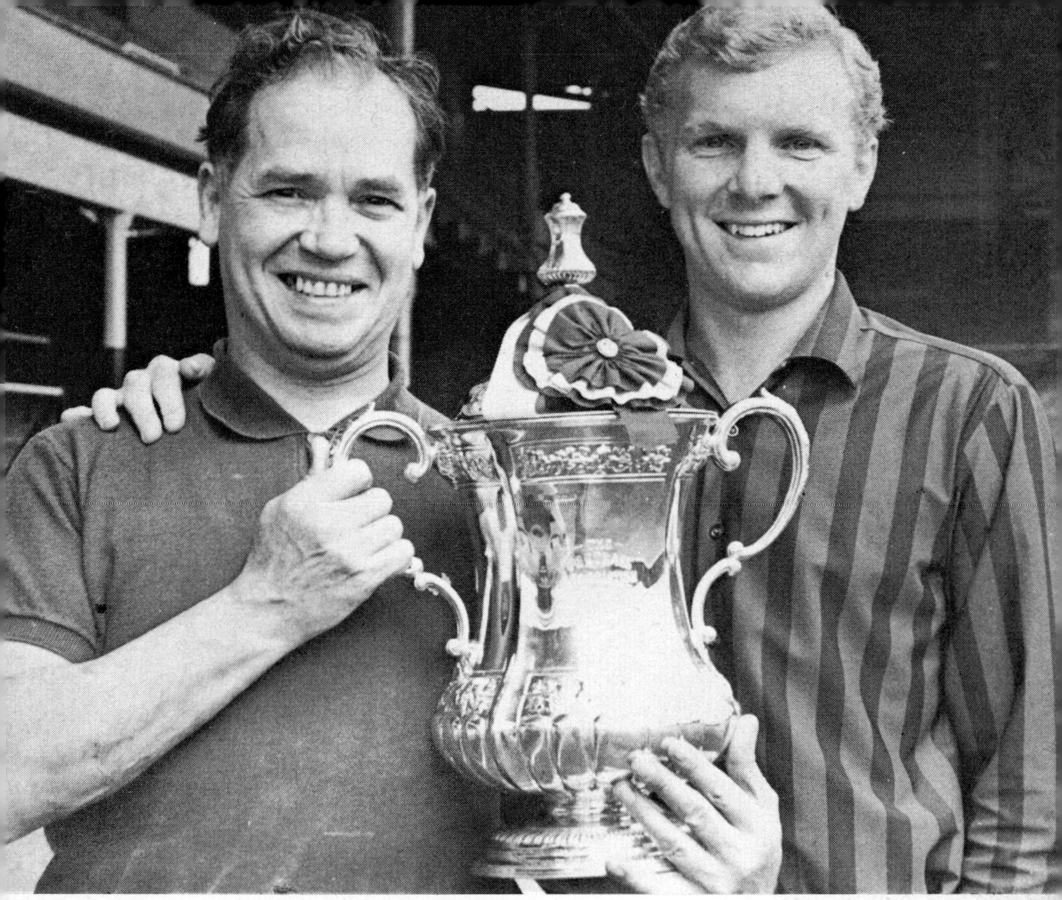

Ee-aye-addio, West Ham's won THE Cup. Bill Jenkins proudly holds the trophy, accompanied by skipper Bobby Moore.

A physiotherapist has to be something of a psychologist and the thinking in soccer has changed to the extent that he is a key figure with the team. Gone are the days when an unconscious player on a cold day was likely to be treated with – a cold sponge. That type of shock treatment is now OUT.

Following Rob's decision to take a player out of action the club doctor comes into the picture. But then it is back to Rob for treatment.

Rob is a quieter personality than his father, of whom he says: 'Dad had a personality that players liked. They could communicate with him.' But West Ham players accord Rob the same respect that his father used to command and his success can be gauged by the volume of callers at his clinic opposite the Upton Park ground.

Players from all over London used to flock to see Bill Jenkins at the clinic when it was over Bobby Moore's sports shop; Bill and Rob decided to move into their own premises in 1966.

Popular full-back John Charles in action against Arsenal at Highbury.

Film star William Holden – 'he thought the world of my Dad', says Rob, and actor Peter Ustinov are but two of the famous from the world of show business who were treated by Bill Jenkins.

When Geoff Hurst had a puzzling back injury some time ago it was Rob Jenkins he turned to for treatment. It was not a specific injury that could be diagnosed, but Geoff was often in pain and Rob spent countless hours at his house treating him and drinking cup after cup of tea.

'He was in pain with that back and I was too,' says Rob.

Martin Peters, Geoff Hurst's World Cup and England colleague, was another player who had trouble with his back. So did Ron Boyce and Jack Burkett, four players from the same era. Rob decided there was a link with something the players had done in their early days at Upton Park.

It is interesting to hear physiotherapist Rob, who knows all the players' secrets from the dressing room, on the West Ham players.

Bobby Ferguson: 'He never gets injured. We did not take a second goalkeeper with us to America last summer because of this. Bobby is never any worry – he's always available to play.'

John Charles: 'He's never bothered by little niggling injuries. I kid him that when he retires we are going to dedicate a plaque in the dressing room to him.'

Billy Bonds: 'He plays even if he is injured. We have a ritual before each match. I always strap his knee for him. It's psychological. If one has it done others want it. Look at the West Ham team next time. You'll see four or five with strapping above their stockings.'

Bobby Howe: 'A most dedicated professional. Bobby has had two cartilages out, one in each knee, and I couldn't praise his attitude any more than I do. He's 100 per cent. I WOULD PUT HIM IN THE SAME CATEGORY AS DAVE MACKAY FOR COURAGE.'

Martin Peters: 'He's my top man for having headaches. On an away trip or when we fly anywhere I always take a few tablets. I never give the players air sickness tablets because it is catching when they start. One of the first team was sick on the way across to America last summer; after we landed several of them complained of feeling ill. Mind you, the present crop of players are good air travellers – not like the bunch that went to the States in 1963 with my father.'

Alan Stephenson: He gets the occasional knock because of the way he plays, but he is no trouble to me.'

Bobby Moore: 'The same – no trouble.'

Harry Redknapp – 'He likes the sun, but it doesn't always like him.

Bobby Howe (*centre*) has the courage of a Dave Mackay, says West Ham physiotherapist Rob Jenkins.

Harry is one of the few sun-worshippers we have in the side, but he is liable to get sunburnt. Luckily there isn't too much sun during our football season.'

Ron Boyce: 'We thought he might be out of football when he had a slipped disc, but he made a splendid recovery.

'He likes a sleeper the night before a game. Ron, John Charles and John Cushley are in the same boat – they can't sleep well without a tablet with a big game approaching.'

Trevor Brooking: 'The lads have nicknamed him "Cyril Lord" – because he is always on the deck! Trevor blisters easily, but he is no bother.'

John Sissons: 'He has made a wonderful recovery after a cartilage operation. He is quite a credit.'

Rob reckons his job would be that much easier if he had a few more Bobby Howes in the camp. He is full of praise for the perseverance of the full-back.

Have the Hammers any idiosyncracies? Nothing more serious, I gather, than Billy Bonds liking a mouthful of water from the sponge each time Rob is called on for treatment. I knew that sponge had some use.

Rob Jenkins, like his father before him, jealously guards his charges. He is proud of the fact that he is the only person Geoff Hurst likes treating his back – 'I feel his back is my property,' he says.

Rob told a well-known M.P. in no uncertain words to 'lay off' when the politician offered Geoff advice on his back trouble.

Not all players earn a bouquet as model patients. Bill Jenkins used to tell the story of the international player he treated painstakingly over a long period after a serious injury – only for the player to break a foot during some horseplay just when he was ready to take his place in the team.

'I have never regretted my decision to give up dentistry to follow my father into football,' says Rob. 'I see the games from a physiotherapy angle and I never comment on tactics or anything like that. We have the Master in Ron Greenwood – that's his job.

'I might miss something vital in a match just because I am watching Geoff Hurst or somebody getting up slowly after a tackle. It may be nothing, but I keep my eyes glued on a player until I am sure he is right and I don't always bother with the play. I get as nervous before a game as the players – but I don't see soccer the same way as them.'

The West Ham players will tell you of Rob Jenkins with his electrical equipment inviting them to the 'threshold of pain'. Some of them complain, but Rob says he does not mind any amount of hollering or shouting so long as the players are available for treatment and keep him in the picture about their injuries.

There is a type, let it be whispered, who is put off by the sight of all the healing equipment in the West Ham dressing rooms and does not come forward to tell of his knocks. Some others are perpetually 'injured', but Rob still spends time checking and treating on a 'Cry Wolf' basis.

He also recalls one first team player, not with West Ham any more, who openly admitted: 'I don't like pain.'

Rob is full of praise for the West Ham club attitude to the players – 'they are not denied anything'. Palmolive soap was brought into the dressing rooms on match days last season because the more normal carbolic caused blemishes in a few cases.

Special soap . . . hair-dressing . . . even after shave lotion. West Ham take no chances when it comes to looking after their charges.

'Sometimes I use kidology on a player to get him to play when I am sure he is fit,' says Rob, 'but the last word on an injury is always with the players.'

Rob Jenkins, who played soccer in the same East Ham district side as Peter Brabrook when he was an East Ham schoolboy, regards Sunday as the most important day of the week for treatment. Every player on the books, from senior down to amateur or schoolboy, is advised to attend the ground for Rob to examine a knock the day after a match.

'It goes right through the club and I try and pay as much attention to a schoolboy as a senior,' says Rob. 'It is essentially a family affair at West Ham, right down to getting treatment.'

Next time you see Rob Jenkins run on to tend an injured player allow for the fact that you are watching an expert at work. His on-the-spot diagnosis can turn a player's career . . . or a match.

Rob is happy following in his father's footsteps, although he has one Wembley appearance to make up. And the West Ham players are happy with Rob, another Jenkins with the 'magic touch' when it comes to healing.

He doesn't make a habit of carrying messages on to the field, but has been known as an authority on the Grand National result in his time!

6

Ron Greenwood

The contribution of Ron Greenwood to soccer as a manager and a coach has earned him accolades from the highest quarters in Britain and abroad. He is a soccer purist . . . a master at his job . . . a candidate for anyone's top ten list of the best in the game.

The West Ham boss – a word he abhors his players using but applicable to his Upton Park status – is also the highest regarded manager in Britain.

I say that without fear of contradiction for, from my own knowledge, I am able to reveal a previously untold story. A First Division club seeking a new manager not so long ago were prepared to offer 48-year-old Ron a £10,000 SIGNING-ON fee to join them which, allied with his ability to name his own terms and negotiate a seven years contract, would have put him in the Herrera class.

In my years around the soccer scene I cannot recall another instance of a manager being wooed with a signing-on fee of that magnitude.

The fact that family man Ron, a regular churchgoer, did not consider the offer is a tribute to his own integrity – when he says that money is not all-important you can believe him – and to the image of West Ham.

Ron is the fourth manager in West Ham's long history, which in itself is a tribute to a great club. He regards his job at Upton Park as the best in football and feels he is working with directors who have an understanding and with players who have the skill and ability to respond.

Ron Greenwood (*left*) in a relaxed mood before a game. Roger Figg, the Barnet goalscorer, shares the joke with Chelsea manager Dave Sexton (*second right*), a former West Ham player, and Arsenal centre-half Ian Ure (*right*).

Not even £10,000 could induce Ron Greenwood to give up the foundations he has created in his eight years at the helm of the family club from East London's dockland area.

As one of the three people who knew the secret I can vouch for the authenticity of the offer and also add that Ron was offered seven years with the rival First Division club to help them 'build on West Ham lines'.

I have known Ron since his playing days. He represents all that is good in soccer – even to turning down £10,000 because of his belief in an ideal.

Listen to his words at the end of last season, a season that can be described as disappointing from a West Ham viewpoint if one discounts the entertainment value of the side that made them as good as any in the land on their day, and the goals sense and flair.

'The whole principle of what we believe in is right,' said Ron. 'The players believe it, the chairman believes it, so do the other directors and so right down to the lowest member of the ground-staff.

'OTHERWISE I COULDN'T CARRY ON.'

West Ham did not win the League championship title. They hovered around the top of the table without making much impact on Leeds, the eventual winners, or Liverpool.

They flattered to deceive in the F.A. Cup. And their defeat at Mansfield against a lowly placed Third Division side was likened to the catastrophe of the 1930s defeat of mighty Arsenal by Walsall, the classic giant-killing act of this century.

I don't subscribe to the view that the Mansfield defeat was in that highly sensational category, but a 3–0 defeat at Field Mill against a side struggling to avoid relegation was a bitter pill. Mansfield won the Cup awarded by the 'Sunday Mirror' as the giant-killers of the season.

As we sat in his well-furnished office at Upton Park, Ron tried to analyse West Ham, 1969, for me and to probe the future.

Are the Hammers too 'flash'? The accusation has been levelled. Is there a degree of arrogance about the wearers of the claret and blue that makes them suspect against lesser mortals . . . Mansfield included? Are they still, as I dubbed their predecessors in an earlier book, gay deceivers?

So much is expected of a side that includes week-in, week-out, three World Cup stars. Ron Greenwood can call on England skipper Bobby Moore, Geoff Hurst, the hat-trick hero of the World Cup Final, and Martin Peters, acknowledged by England team manager, Sir Alf Ramsey, as the best player of his type in the world.

Ron Greenwood coaching the first team squad at Upton Park. He favours the simple things in soccer.

So what does Ron Greenwood say ? He told me: 'Well, our club is certainly well-organised. There isn't a better-run club in the country. We produce two players a year for our first team.

'It's a darned elusive question for the fact is that we haven't won anything. Let me say that I don't remember the past – I remember the future. I don't look back – in football the next day is the important one.

'Because one suffers silently people imagine that you don't feel pain or anguish, but this is not true. The fact is that all of us at Upton Park have this utter belief in what we are trying to do.'

Have West Ham got their heads in a cloud ? Can a team that puts an emphasis on attack and the purity of its football survive at the very top against the Method sides with their professionalism and their defensive tactics ?

Ron Greenwood shrugs aside the argument. 'We are not idealistic,' he says. 'We are realistic. I am sure the fans like the way the club plays. The crowds still turn up to see us, whether we are winning the League or not. The fact that we have enjoyed our best-ever crowd aggregate for a season proves, surely, that the fans believe with us that what we are attempting is correct.'

So what of the future ? Must we followers of the Hammers accept a secondary role and satisfy ourselves with the knowledge that we are better than those that edge us out at the top ?

There is no defeatism from Ron Greenwood. 'We want to win this great championship of England – but win it the way we believe. This is no discredit to Leeds, but we would like to win it because everybody wants us to.'

I am sure that is a fact. Everton manager Harry Catterick has gone on record as saying that he would like his team to win playing the type of attacking game that entertains as well as gains success – and his team have gained many admirers.

The Hammers can do it because they have such wonderful flair. But will they do it ?

THE MISSING LINK

Ron Greenwood came up with an interesting theory that I am sure will draw nods of approval from all with West Ham interests at heart.

He told me: 'Somewhere along the line we are short of one elusive ingredient. I have got to find out what that is.

'I don't think we need someone to kick a bit. It is a question of finding someone in the right department to turn the whole issue. Like Johnny Byrne did for us when we got among the honours earlier in the 1960s. Vic Keeble did it for the side before I came to West Ham.'

So, the search is on for a Keeble or a Byrne. The missing link. The inspiration that will carry the Hammers to fresh triumphs . . . and delight fans from Merseyside to Elland Road.

The fact that Ron mentioned Keeble, whose golden goals helped the Hammers from Second to First Divisions, and Byrne, the di Stefano of the English game in his prime, suggests the required ingredient for success could be in attack. Certainly the Hammers were tighter at the back in season 1968–9 than at any time since the war.

'No one does more soul-searching than me,' Ron told me. 'In my heart of hearts I know what we want . . . I am sure I know what we want. I think it is in the same department as before.

'There are so many amateur critics who are willing to tell us what we want, but the outsider has no conception of what the game is about internally.

'I am not decrying people who watch and criticise. That's what the game is about – opinion. But to tell us we need so-and-so, or a player in a certain position, is all nonsense.

'The players have all got to have an affinity. They have got to hate each other or hate the manager – something like that, something in common.

'We have an affinity at West Ham . . . an affinity in skill and being good guys. The affinity missing is the sparking plug to success.'

Ron drew the comparison of two England players in the World Cup winning side of 1966 who argued fiercely with each other and blended to soccer success.

'It's indefinable where it is missing with us, this spark,' he said. 'But it has got to be found.'

The inference, of course, is a splurge into the transfer market to find the link, but Ron added: 'He could spring from here. He could be one of the emerging players already at Upton Park, one who could spring to the forefront following our tour to America last summer.'

Ron is aware of the critics who say that the wrong team is picked each Saturday. He knows the shouts that go up when the team fails to score goals. But, as a wise manager of experience, he keeps his counsel on these matters and reasons that West Ham are sound physically and in tactics. They ARE well organised.

I asked him to break his rule and look back. How did he see the 1968–9 season?

'Now, I want you all to listen carefully to what I've got to say. . . .'

'I want you to take their centre-forward. . . .'

'One cannot be satisfied,' he replied. 'Obviously it was a disappointment, a frustrating season. We achieved so much, but with nothing to show for it.'

In two years with Bobby Ferguson in goal, and with the advent of Alan Stephenson, the goals-against column has come down. 'What we have further achieved is in our own belief in ourselves,' he said.

'We know we can match the best. Looking back on the season we know we have played well, although towards the end of the season we stopped scoring goals, which generally is the easiest thing for us.'

One of the highlights of the season for the Upton Park fans was the 8–0 defeat of Sunderland, the day Geoff Hurst scored six goals.

'We scored eight that day,' says Ron, 'but we should have beaten Sheffield Wednesday 20–0. Instead we drew 1–1. There were more draws last season than I have ever known. Many of those at Upton Park were because people came to play us who were scared to death of us.

'Some of the away draws were good results, but there were other games we should have won.'

After the shock Cup defeat by Mansfield, Ron Greenwood told me: 'I am still hurt, and will be for a long time.'

‘All we’ve got to do is keep calm. . . .’

‘and we’ll cut their defence to ribbons.’

‘Our aim is to win the League Championship playing the West Ham way.’

Days after losing at Field Mill, the Hammers played Newcastle at home and beat the Inter Cities Fairs Cup finalists 3–1 after scoring two goals in the first 13 minutes. They shrugged off the Cup memory with a typically bright display.

Ron said at the time that the Hammers played better in the first 20 minutes at Mansfield than they did against Newcastle, a statement that took some believing for those of us who only saw the one game.

'We have never been better prepared for a game than the visit to Mansfield,' said Ron in retrospect. 'We approached it in a better way than I remember for any game of my time here. Unfortunately, Geoff Hurst missed an open goal at a vital time . . . and it was never to be. I must be philosophical about it. We were so tense and keen that things didn't flow easily.

'No one could be accused of lack of effort. Mansfield deserved their win; they raised their game.

'If that defeat is as big a disaster as Walsall beating Arsenal, well all I can say is that I take it as a COMPLIMENT to West Ham.'

Ron Greenwood does get hurt. He guards the reputations of his players with almost fatherly care and rarely reveals his innermost feelings to the outside world. I can tell you of two further disappointments to him during the 1968–9 season, West Ham's first away defeats.

'We were caught with our pants down against a young Burnley side,' he said. 'We could have equalised, but didn't and had to accept defeat.'

'Then we went to Leeds determined to do well. We played well and we really had something at stake that afternoon. We played attacking football, our brand of soccer at its best.

'The sending-off of Harry Redknapp at Leeds was the most disappointing thing that happened to us all season, added to which was the penalty award gained by Billy Bremner for the home side.'

It did not help when Bremner, who came third in the annual Footballer of the Year poll, went on television some time later to applaud West Ham's attacking style. 'They let you play,' was his verdict – one that we have heard before often enough. Is it a compliment or a back-handed compliment? West Ham are more liable to win 4–3 than draw 0–0; you won't find many 4–3 results in the champions' list.

'I am continually hurt by our lack of success. This club deserves to succeed,' Ron told me.

There is probably only one other person who knows Ron as well as he knows himself, his wife, Lucy.

She has told me: 'His devotion to his players is frightening at times. I wonder if they ever realise it. He is very fair to them.'

Ron Greenwood never runs down his team. As an ex-professional – he played for Chelsea, Bradford, Brentford and Fulham – he has respect for each and every one of them.

Ron says: 'I defend my players along the line. Because I am not always shouting my head off people think I don't care – but I probably care more than those who shout the loudest.'

Goalkeepers Peter Grotier and Steve Death were blooded in the West Ham first team at the tail-end of the 1968–9 season. So was young Pat Holland. Jamaican Clyde Best made his mark on the club's American trip.

So the pipeline that has produced Moore, Hurst and Peters, to name the outstanding three of the current crop, is still functioning.

Waiting in the wings at Upton Park is inside forward Jimmy Lindsay, the Scottish youth international of whom Ron Greenwood says: 'We have great hopes for him.'

Full back Frank Lampard is back after breaking a leg – 'he showed great spirit and determination,' says Ron Greenwood – and Bobby Howe, who was in West Ham's Youth Cup winning side of 1963, made an impact in the first team. 'Bobby emerged as a first team player through patience and all that is good in soccer,' says Ron.

Will the missing link that Ron Greenwood seeks come from the youth ranks ? From a Best or a Lindsay ? Only time will tell – I know, though, that there is the same dedicated approach to soccer and soccer skills that there has always been in recent years. Thirteen Hammers players took a coaching course last season – and all passed.

West Ham is not, of course, a one-man show. Former goalkeeper Ernie Gregory has established himself as a coach at Upton Park, and 30-year-old John Lyall, the full-back whose playing career was terminated by injury, has gulfed the gap between playing and coaching to become youth team manager.

'I think John will figure highly in West Ham's plans for the future – or some other club's plans,' says Ron.

The West Ham manager – the senior players call him 'Ron', the youngsters 'Mr. Greenwood' – has always been to the forefront in soccer thinking.

He was a Football Association staff coach at Lilleshall preaching the virtues of the 4–2–4 formation when former West Ham players Malcolm Allison (now coach to Cup winning Manchester City) and Dave Sexton (now managing Chelsea) attended.

Jimmy Andrews (now coach to Luton) and Noel Cantwell (manager of Coventry these days) followed up – and the coaching bug was carried back to Upton Park.

It is a tribute to West Ham that so many of their 'old boys' have made their way in the game as managers or coaches.

Allison and Malcolm Musgrove (Leicester City) were the coaches of last season's Cup Finalists. Frank O'Farrell, another ex-Hammer, managed Leicester.

Sexton . . . Cantwell . . . Jimmy Barrett (now with Q.P.R.). The list goes on. Phil Woosnam is executive director of the North American Soccer League.

In his eight years at Upton Park, Ron Greenwood has spent £338,000 on players – and the sale of Brian Dear to Fulham early in 1969 enabled him to balance the books. 'I am a steady person with my money and the club's,' says Ron.

Lancashire-born Ron – he learned to play football wearing the clogs of his native county – is the son of a painter. He was apprenticed to a firm of signwriters as a boy – and some of his signs are still on the doors at Wembley Stadium today.

The major influences on his soccer thinking were Billy Birrell, the former Chelsea manager, Malcolm MacDonald, who was the trainer at Brentford when Ron was a player there, former England team manager Walter Winterbottom and Arthur Rowe, whose push-and-run style helped Spurs to win the Second and First Division titles.

Ron Greenwood has an uncomplicated approach to coaching. He favours the basic simple things he has drilled into him, although he says: 'Simplicity in soccer is hard.'

At West Ham the players play the game Ron Greenwood always wanted to play. He says he is lucky to have the players who can do it the way he wants.

They played it the Greenwood way to win the Youth Cup in 1963, the F.A. Cup in 1964 and the European Cup Winners' Cup in 1965. 'Everything we believed in came true in that match,' he said.

His wife has told me that Ron's love of soccer is consuming – 'almost like a light shining' – and I believe that this young-at-heart grandfather will inspire further success for the Hammers.

When he finds his missing link.

Don't tell Alan

The fan who walked up to Alan Stephenson in the forecourt at Tottenham last season after the Hammers had lost 1–0 said the wrong thing.

'Unlucky again,' was his comment – but those two words rankled. Particularly the 'again'. And I would strongly advise against repetition of the sentiment to 25-year-old Stephenson, a quiet-spoken six-footer on the exterior but a footballer with a hard, determined streak beating beneath the surface.

That defeat at Tottenham typified West Ham's disappointing finish to the 1968–9 season. They didn't score goals in the run-in and, although they got their usual glowing write-ups in the newspapers after most of the games, the fact that they were lost hit Alan Stephenson and Co.

I know how he feels. Leeds skipper Billy Bremner, safe in the knowledge that his team had clinched the League championship title for the first time, acknowledged West Ham's skill in an interview on television.

'They let you play,' he said. Such is the current reputation of the Hammers – they let other teams play good football. Bremner meant, of course, that the majority of their championship rivals favoured more of a defensive outlook in a bid to stop Leeds.

Alan Stephenson sees it as very much a back-handed compliment. The most expensive signing in the history of the Hammers – he cost £80,000 from Crystal Palace on 12 March 1968 – told me: 'We have got to destroy this image.'

Not that Stephenson is advocating a move from the footballing principles that makes West Ham so admired. 'We have got to do it on the park,' he emphasises. 'We have got to win the First Division playing the West Ham way – we have got to prove that we are right.'

Fighting words. Yet words that will meet with approval far beyond the confines of Upton Park.

'It will be a good thing for football if West Ham can win the League title playing the way we do,' says Stephenson. 'Until we do we can't really say that what we are trying to do is 100 per cent right.'

Alan was born at Chesham, Bucks, but brought up in Walthamstow. His elder brother, Norman, played centre-half or wing-half for the Avenue, the famous Isthmian League amateurs, and Alan followed in his footballing footsteps by captaining the Walthamstow district boys side. Eventually he was chosen to play for London.

That's where Arthur Rowe, one of soccer's finest judges, stepped in. Arthur, architect of the push-and-run style that took Spurs to the League championship title in the 1950s, was managing Crystal Palace at the time. He liked what he saw of young Stephenson playing for London against Glasgow at Stamford Bridge.

Arthur Rowe wrote to Alan's school-teacher and received permission for the youngster to attend Selhurst Park for trials. In the summer of 1961 Alan was asked to play for the Palace youth side in the South-East Counties League.

A few games followed in the reserves and Alan was asked to sign professional forms. He said: 'NO.'

Politely, of course, but firmly. The main reason was that he had been turned down by Leyton Orient, the team he had supported as a boy when Sid Bishop was the centre-half, and he had doubts.

'I wasn't certain that I could make the grade,' he says. 'I told Arthur Rowe I was more interested in a job and that I preferred to remain an amateur.'

Odd for a player who was to win recognition at England Under–23 level and command the attention and respect of such a shrewd judge as West Ham manager Ron Greenwood.

But Alan was firm – and Palace signed him as a part-time player in February 1962, his father's birthday. He combined soccer with a job in the circulation department of *The Times*.

Alan made his League debut for Palace the following month, a 0–0 draw at Selhurst against Bradford Park Avenue. The following season he decided he stood a chance as a League player and became a full-time professional.

From this uncertain beginning Alan progressed to some 170 senior

Leeds skipper Billy Bremner says of West Ham: 'They let you play.'

games for Palace and three caps for the Under–23 side, the first of these in October 1966 in a side that beat Wales 8–0 at Wolverhampton.

Brian Wood and Gwyn Evans were the centre-half rivals to up-and-coming Stephenson at Selhurst Park, but he played 26 games in the side that won promotion from the Third Division in season 1963–4. His role was at wing-half alongside Wood, a dual centre-half tactic that was a basis for Palace's rise to the Second Division. When Wood was unlucky enough to break a leg Alan switched to his usual centre-half position – and made it his own.

'Arthur Rowe, who was a centre-half in his playing days before the war, was a great influence on me,' says Alan. 'He is on Ron Greenwood lines, or should that be the other way round? They both talk to you and listen to what you have to say – you feel you are talking to a father or an uncle.'

Palace coach George Petchey was another influence on the development of Stephenson, who was linked with Wolves when wing-half John Holsgrove was transferred to the Molineux club. Apparently Dick Graham, manager of Palace at the time, was not keen on losing two wing-halves, so Stephenson stayed.

West Ham moved in at £70,000 for Stephenson early in 1967 – but it was another year before Ron Greenwood got his man and the price was an extra £10,000.

'I had told Palace I was interested in playing First Division football and my choice for the England Under–23 side hardened my resolve to get into the top class,' says Alan.

A year elapsed between Alan's first Under–23 call and his second, a 1–0 defeat of Italy at Nottingham. Ron Greenwood watched him gain his third cap, against Scotland.

'I understood that West Ham had an option on me after their initial enquiry in 1967,' says Alan. 'Anyway, in March 1968 I was called into the manager's office at Palace and told that they had made a bid. I was pleased with this. I had always thought of West Ham as a very good side and there was nowhere I would rather have gone.'

After talks with Ron Greenwood and a 24 hours deliberation, Alan signed for the Hammers. Ron Greenwood told him: 'If you do as well with us as the last player we took from Palace you will be doing well.'

He referred, of course, to Johnny ('Budgie') Byrne, the former England centre-forward who later returned to Palace and subsequently moved to Fulham and on to South Africa.

How did Stephenson find the West Ham 'family' when he arrived at Upton Park with the tag of being the most expensive player in the history of the club?

'The club as a whole made me friendly,' he says. 'The feeling of being wanted was a big thing as far as I was concerned – I found the spirit very good.'

Surprisingly good considering that West Ham had just been knocked out of the Cup by Sheffield United and the League position was little to write home about.

Alan recalls: 'I was so over the moon at signing that I didn't realise how far down the League we were.'

He made twelve First Division appearances at the end of the 1968–9 season and then gained a further three England Under–23 caps during the England tour of Europe that summer.

West Ham Manager Ron Greenwood – signed Alan Stephenson for a club record fee of £80,000.

'I was quite surprised by the standard of play when I made my early outings in the First Division,' Alan says. 'There are such good players around.

'Mind you, I was more surprised at the quality of West Ham. I hadn't appreciated to the full until I played with the side what ability and skill there was at the club. In the First Division if you haven't got a grip on the midfield other teams can cut you to ribbons.

'Some people talk about the physical contact of the First Division. I don't agree – it's as hard in the First as it is in the Second and Third Divisions. It is harder to get the ball as a defender in the First because the passing is so much better. You have to win it all the time.'

The Upton Park regulars accepted Alan Stephenson at face value and made him feel as much a part of the scene as his team-mates had done when he arrived.

He says: 'I didn't worry about the transfer fee that was paid for me. I accepted it. I was bought by West Ham for a purpose and they believed in me enough to pay that sort of money. I felt I must give 100 per cent in determination every game in return – that's what I do.'

Alan is grateful for the help he received from his colleagues when he slotted into a side that, at the time, had a reputation for giving away too many 'soft' goals.

'Bobby Moore and Billy Bonds are so good – they have made life easier for me,' says Alan.

Well, the impact of Alan Stephenson certainly made itself felt last season. Study the West Ham goals against columns since the club returned to the First Division in 1958–9 – 70, 91, 86, 82, 69, 74, 71, 83, 84 and 69. Last season's figures reduced that by 19, a best-ever defensive total since the war of 50.

Twelve-stone Alan – 'I've put on weight since I left Palace for the Hammers' – has matured as a player and a person at Upton Park. Part of the credit, he says, goes to his wife, Marion, who is a keen supporter. They married in June 1968.

Alan rates Welsh international Ron Davies, the Southampton centre-forward, as the most lethal opponent he has met in the First Division, and he lists Brian Labone, Everton's England international, as the ideal centre-half – 'he's very cool and very efficient'.

His biggest soccer thrill? Signing for the Hammers, although he also highlights a fifth round Cup defeat of Nottingham Forest before a record Selhurst crowd when he was a Palace player. Alan marked Frank Wignall, now of Derby, and Palace won 3–1.

Last season's Cup defeat at Mansfield ranks as Alan's blackest

Crystal Palace assistant manager Arthur Rowe, pictured at home with his wife. He invited Alan Stephenson for trials at Selhurst Park.

moment in soccer - I assure him he is not alone in sharing the horrible memory – but life at West Ham has had far more ups than downs for him.

As a player who had received his training in the lower Divisions he relished the new places and new faces of the top grade. 'I enjoyed playing at Manchester United and at Liverpool, although we lost there. What fantastic supporters they have at Anfield – they give a game so much atmosphere.'

Alan – 'I am a very quiet person, I don't have a lot to say' – has been impressed by the warmth of the crowd at Upton Park and speaks highly of the atmosphere at home games.

Alan enjoys all sports, squash, badminton and table tennis. He plays cricket for Walthamstow in the summer and has scored a few runs in his time. He likes travelling, particularly to Spain. The heat appeals to him.

What has being a West Ham player taught him? The answer is not surprising, although the reasons may be.

'I have learned about losing my rag in a game,' he says. 'I used to have a go at myself – let my emotions come out. I still tend to get annoyed, but I have learned control since arriving at West Ham. I realise that you cannot change a referee's decision, so what's the use of blowing your top and getting into trouble? I feel much better with this outlook – you are in control of yourself once you learn the lesson and it can only help your play because you are in control.'

I presumed it was West Ham indoctrination that had swung Stephenson to this way of thinking. But, no . . .

'I've matured as a person, perhaps it's being married,' he says.

His major ambition, one that will get a 'hear, hear' from all of us with the claret and blue at heart, is for the Hammers to win the First Division title.

Stephenson coaches a youth side, Highams Park, on Tuesday nights and applies the simple philosophy: 'They seem to enjoy my doing it – I like doing it.'

An uncomplicated person is Alan Stephenson. He has added backbone to the West Ham defence by his presence and, taking his words at face value, he is dedicated to helping the club to fresh triumphs. He, like many of us, wants the other teams playing the West Ham way. But he wants the results to match the plaudits.

Crystal Palace manager Bert Head has said he bought several players for his promotion-winning team with the money he received from West Ham for Alan.

It's an odd fact of soccer life that Alan helped Palace on the way to

Alan Stephenson – a quiet six-footer on the exterior, but a footballer with a hard determined streak beneath the surface.

the First Division by his transfer; I prefer to think, as I told him, that they needed six players to replace him!

Don't tell Alan that West Ham are unlucky – ever again. Or the quiet man might suddenly become vocal. I am sure those emotions he now bottles up will rise to the surface when the Hammers gain more success – still letting their opponents play soccer.

Bobby Ferguson

Goalkeepers, they say, don't have to be mad – but it helps. By that reckoning Scottish international Bobby Ferguson, who cost West Ham a world record fee for a goalkeeper of £60,000, should at least be a roaring extrovert.

Far from it. Bobby, who I have known since he was an up and coming youngster with Scottish First Division club Kilmarnock, is a modest, unassuming chap. The tag of being the priciest goalkeeper in soccer history does not weigh heavily on his shoulders . . . he does not brood over lost goals . . . he does not indulge in histrionics of any sort.

He is, in his own words, 'a normal bloke'; a professional who enjoys the life of a soccer star but is unaffected by the adulation and the trimmings.

Bobby can also be a severe critic of his own play. In a bout of self-analysis he told me: 'I don't shout enough on the field. I am not bossy enough. I've got to make myself shout and be bossy.'

West Ham have been noted for the quality of their home-grown products. They spread the net over 400 miles when they brought Bobby Ferguson into 'the family'.

He comes from Ardrossan, Ayrshire, which he irreverently describes as a quiet spot 'with fourteen pubs and a bingo hall'. Back home in Scotland, Bobby was reared on a diet of rugby football – and he didn't like that one bit.

At school he was a three-quarter for a few games – 'I didn't fancy it' – and his escape from the compulsory game was to play for the local Boys' Brigade soccer team at centre-half.

The story of how he became an international goalkeeper and then the highest priced in the land is told in the simplest terms. One day the Boys' Brigade goalie was injured – and Bobby was called on to deputise.

'I was the biggest fellow in the team, so I went in,' he recalls. 'I preferred playing on the park, but I stayed in as goalkeeper and became the regular.'

That twist of fortune led to his being noticed by a Kilmarnock scout when he was fourteen, and Bobby joined Kilmarnock Amateurs. At the age of 17 he reported to Rugby Park, Kilmarnock's home ground, for Tuesday and Thursday evening training sessions, and eventually he made his debut in the reserve side.

From a £7-a-week start Bobby shot up the soccer ladder with startling rapidity. Willie Waddell, the former Glasgow Rangers and Scotland winger who was managing Killies at the time, had faith in the youngster he had signed and he replaced Campbell Forsyth, Scotland's No. 1 choice for a time, in the club first eleven.

Bobby had made a handful of appearances in the Scottish First Division when, at the age of 20, he was called up for the first of his seven international caps. He took over from Bill Brown, the former Tottenham goalkeeper, in the Scotland side.

Despite his meteoric rise, Bobby was happy at Kilmarnock, which is only 16 miles from his home town, but the wages paid north of the border do not compare with those paid in the Football League and pretty soon there were a 'few whispers'.

West Ham manager Ron Greenwood, seeking a front-rank goalkeeper, travelled to watch Kilmarnock play in a Fairs' Cup tie. He spoke to his friend, Malcolm MacDonald, who had succeeded Willie Waddell as Kilmarnock boss, and eventually a fee was agreed.

I remember travelling to Glasgow on a business trip and going to Parkhead with Kilmarnock for an away game against Celtic. Ron Greenwood was there – watching Ferguson, and also a centre-half in the Celtic side named John Cushley.

Celtic, then at their peak, won the match 2–0, but the result would have been considerably more but for the brilliance of Ferguson. The Celtic attack helped him turn on a display that was flawless.

When Malcolm MacDonald, who was at Brentford with Ron Greenwood in their playing days, and was a mentor to the West Ham manager, asked Bobby if he wished to join the Hammers, the answer was a quick 'Yes'.

West Ham was a name to him, but he studied their results and came to the conclusion he was being linked with a top club although,

Bobby Ferguson – at £60,000 the costliest goalkeeper in the world.

as he says, 'all they know up there is Manchester United and Spurs'.

Wages were discussed on the telephone and finally Ron Greenwood travelled North again to sign Bobby after a Fairs' Cup tie at Rugby Park against Leeds.

Moving to London was not such a problem for Bobby as for most bachelor imports for he had relatives living at Shadwell by the River Thames – they are now at Basildon – and the problem of 'digs' was solved.

I asked Bobby how it felt to be a £60,000 goalkeeper with the label 'the costliest in the world'. He was unconcerned.

'It's the managers who make the fee – it was nothing to do with me', he replied. 'It certainly didn't worry me, although I took time to settle at Upton Park.

'In fact, I am still settling.'

As an 'outsider' when he joined the Hammers on 25 May 1967 – there were only three Scots on the books at the time – he has nothing but praise for the Hammers. 'A great club', he enthuses. 'They really look after you and everything about West Ham is above board. We have a good bunch of lads at Upton Park . . . there are no cliques'.

Bobby is now 24 and has had experience at top level in Scotland and England. With Kilmarnock he won Scottish League and Reserve Cup medals and, following eight Scotland Youth caps, he gained two Scottish League calls before his international debut.

'Scottish football is entirely different,' he says. 'The game is not faster down here, but it is harder and more skilful. A goalkeeper finds he meets skilful players week in and week out, and that presents more problems.'

Skill? He rates George Best and club colleague Geoff Hurst at the top of the tree, although he rarely has to face the fire and power shooting of Hurst. Bobby plays on the field whenever he can in practice matches.

West Ham coach Ernie Gregory, a goalkeeper of distinction himself, has been an influence on Ferguson. 'He helped me on angles . . . . I wasn't doing it right when I moved down from Scotland. Ernie has got me thinking.'

Manager Greenwood, who was impressed by the qualities of instinctiveness of 5ft. 11in. Ferguson, has been a help to Bobby in ironing out mistakes, and has developed his attitude of mind to the game.

It is no secret that Ferguson has had his detractors and critics in London and some of his mistakes have been magnified. As Bobby says: 'I got a lot of stick from the Press, which used to bother me. Not

Bobby Ferguson punches clear from Liverpool's Alun Evans during a First Division match at Upton Park in February 1969. John Charles (*left*) looks on.

Bobby Ferguson chasing a loose ball. He was reared on a diet of rugby football.

now. Ron Greenwood has helped my outlook.

'There has been surprisingly little reaction from the West Ham crowd. They could have laid it on a few times – they haven't'.

Ron Greenwood, who chose Bobby Ferguson because of his youth in preference to England World Cup goalkeeper Gordon Banks, who was available at the time and under consideration by West Ham, defended his choice when the critics were noisy at one time. 'He's got years ahead of him,' he pointed out.

I became involved in a few verbal battles with the anti-Ferguson brigade who, I feel, expected superhuman things from Bobby because of his price tag.

Banks, incidentally, is a goalkeeper who earns the highest accolade from Ferguson. Chelsea's Peter Bonetti is the other . . . ironically another 'keeper who might have joined West Ham at one stage.

Bobby's most satisfying match as a West Ham player was the 3–1 victory against Burnley at Turf Moor in the third-round of the F.A. Cup in 1968. That made up for a previous League appearance at the Burnley ground – 'I lost a goal and played a stinker'.

Bobby refuses to brood over bad performances. Like all good professionals, he hates to lose – but his attitude is that all the brooding in the world will not right the scoreline and all he can do is try and remedy mistakes next time.

His nightmare experience was at the Hawthorns in the 1967–8 season when West Bromwich Albion whipped the Hammers 3–0, 'three bad goals,' he recalls.

I reckon Bobby's reflexes are his strongest point as a goalkeeper, and recall a double-barrelled save he made from Irish international Derek Dougan at Molineux last season to back the point. Dougan fired in a shot – Bobby saved . . . then stopped the rebound shot going the other way.

Bobby's hobbies are collecting records and swimming. He was married in May 1968, to an Australian girl, Greer, he met at a cafe in Scotland when she was visiting relatives north of the border and the Fergusons live in a detached house at Upminster.

West Ham, being the club it is, has adopted Ferguson, Scottish accent and all. 'The Cockneys kid me all the time, but we get on well,' says Bobby.

He travels home for a week or so in the summer and tries to get to Scotland for the New Year celebrations. If he wasn't a footballer – he completed a five years' apprenticeship as an engineer and won certificates – Bobby might have emigrated to Australia by now. Greer's parents are there. He plans to resume his engineering studies as a safeguard for when his playing days are over.

That's Bobby Ferguson, weighing in at 12 stone and with a spring-heeled walk. Unworried by the critics and determined to do his best and prove Ron Greenwood right.

The tragedy for both Ferguson and fellow Scot John Cushley, the £20,000 centre-half the Hammers signed to replace long-serving Ken

Brown, was that they failed to strike an immediate understanding. The play of both suffered in their early days at Upton Park, although Ron Greenwood insisted that neither player was to blame.

Ron Greenwood has been at Upton Park for eight years now and he reckons he is a new boy. Well, Bobby Ferguson has a mere two seasons behind him and he has youth on his side as he tries to prove a worthy successor to Ted Hufton, Ernie Gregory and Co.

Bobby reckons he is still settling in. I wager that when he does he'll have few 'stinkers' and fewer 'bad goals' to recall.

Perhaps he'll help establish West Ham to the extent that the folk 407 miles away in Ardrossan rate them in the super class alongside Manchester United and Spurs.

Reg Pratt Believes in the Family Image

Reg Pratt, chairman of West Ham United since 1950, summed up his football philosophy to me in this crisp sentence: 'I am still a square. Football is the greatest team game in the world and I believe that it should be played in the right spirit.'

You can take it from me that West Ham will not deviate one jot from the course they set down, to play entertaining and sporting football, even if it means forfeiting the chance of a League Championship title.

Let them all play the West Ham way, I wrote in a previous West Ham book. That's what I would like to see – even if it seems an unrealistic thought in these days when a multitude of soccer sins are covered by the word 'professionalism'.

Mr. Pratt decries all that comes under the heading of gamesmanship in the modern game. He goes further and talks of clubs 'cheating to win'.

Well, West Ham won't be joining the herd. The emphasis on the game at Upton Park will remain on attacking football and an unswerving belief in ideals laid down well over half a century ago.

Let me record Mr. Pratt's own words as he sat, reflectively sucking at his favourite pipe, and pondered my question on how ambitious the Hammers were to climb to the top of Soccer's Everest and joust with the Method sides of the late 1960s for the coveted Championship title.

'We shall follow our ideals to the bitter end,' he replied. 'It is

Reg Pratt, the West Ham chairman, who says: 'We will never sacrifice our ideals.'

nice to finish high in the League table, but we will never decide that because we are nearly there we should throw everything in which we believe to the winds and resort to tactics alien to our beliefs.

'We have proved that one can win trophies without resorting to gamesmanship or cheating. To have proved it at UNESCO level was really something.'

That United Nations trophy for Fair Play, awarded to West Ham the season they stormed to victory in the European Cup Winners' Cup, gave the genial Mr. Pratt more pleasure than seeing Bobby Moore going first to the rostrum as the victorious skipper.

Reg Pratt, a 64-year-old company director and timber merchant, is no hypocrite campaigning for the ideals of Fair Play and Sport. He was a Justice of the Peace at East Ham for 25 years and is imbued with the principles he preaches.

When he says 'We would not tolerate dirty play at West Ham' you accept the words – even if it meant losing a League title by sticking to the principle.

Mr. Pratt may be a square to the moderns in his pin-stripe suits. They may scoff at his thinking on sport as Victorian in an era where to finish as runner-up is to fail. But, by golly, they had better believe that he means what he says.

Talk to Reg Pratt, as I have on several occasions, and you become imbued with his fanaticism for the West Ham ideals. It is easy to see why West Ham have had only four managers this century, and to trace the origins of any success the club has had.

Reg Pratt was brought up in a West Ham environment. His father was a lifelong supporter, a local man who was a fanatical follower of the Hammers. As a young man he went to see his doctor complaining of being unwell AFTER he had been to football one afternoon and found that he was suffering from scarlet fever!

Mr. Pratt, senior, was chairman of the Boleyn Castle Sports Club which used to be adjacent to the Upton Park ground and, with a common membership and his long association, it was not surprising that he was invited to join the West Ham Board in 1923. He received a gold medal after the first Wembley Cup Final.

Eventually Frank Pratt became vice-chairman to his lifelong friend, W. J. (Will) Cearns – a link that is maintained on the Board to the present day.

West Ham have always gloried in a family club image, and the histories at Upton Park of the Pratt and Cearns families bear a testimony to the tradition. J. W. (Jimmy) Cearns was a committeeman of Thames Ironworks, F.C., the forerunner of West Ham, and he became a director when the present club was formed. One of his sons was Will Cearns, the former chairman.

Will Cearns and Frank Pratt joined the Board together and, when Mr. Pratt died in December 1940, Reg Pratt was invited to take his place. He succeeded Will Cearns as chairman on his death in 1950.

In the meantime, West Ham had co-opted Len Cearns to the Board, and he was later joined by his brothers, Will and Brian, all third generation supporters and directors.

'It's not nepotism,' argues Reg Pratt. 'It is a form of recruitment of men trained for the job. The Pratts and the Cearns families are imbued with the West Ham club and ideals. It's an apprenticeship for the job. Yes, job. For, after all, it is a job of work. I spend a lot of time dealing with West Ham business. You can't play at being a director of a football club. It's a big responsibility – not all fun and games by any means. You can't let up. You certainly can't sit back and say, "We have arrived." In soccer you have to think some three to five years ahead all the time. And you have to learn from the mistakes of others.'

Reg Pratt believes in the family image and tradition. He was brought up in the atmosphere of the Hammers, as were the Cearns brothers. 'You regard it as a heritage – it is something put in your trust to carry on the traditions laid down many years ago,' he says.

As a seven-year-old Reg Pratt paid his sixpence and watched the Hammers from the terraces. Later he remembers his father talking about West Ham from 'the inside'.

He contends all this is good for the club. 'It's very valuable. You absorb if you come on to the scene early enough and bide your time. You absorb tradition and get the feel for policies to such an extent that you want to carry them on.'

The family tradition is not confined to the directors' room. Will Cearns' brother, Frank, an ex-referee, was the West Ham secretary before Eddie Chapman. Other members of the Cearns family are voluntary workers at Upton Park on match days – as are the sons of former manager Charlie Paynter. Then there is the Helliar family, who have been the club's printers from the start. Third generation Jack Helliar is the present Programme Editor, and he is training his son.

Reg Pratt contends: 'There are so many people who are second or third generation associated with West Ham that there is continuity of a deep interest.'

THE HERITAGE

When Charlie Paynter's playing career with West Ham was prematurely ended by injury in 1902 he was out of soccer for many months. When the Hammers moved to their present ground Charlie was put in charge of the reserve side – and that began an era that led to all that is good at the club.

When I asked Reg Pratt about the heritage of the Hammers, he replied: 'In my personal opinion we can thank Charlie Paynter. He began to wield a strong influence when he took over.'

At that stage in soccer history players are far removed from the jet-set era of unrestricted wages. In Reg Pratt's words they were 'a different breed'.

There was more of a cloth cap and choker image about the professional footballer of the early 1900s – and Charlie Paynter's first edict in his staff role at Upton Park was startling. 'Everyone of you wears a collar and tie from now on,' he decreed 'and there will be no bad language.'

'Charlie was a stickler,' says Reg Pratt with pride. 'He made the players respectable. He even stopped them playing cards in the dressing-rooms – and there was nearly a revolution!'

This was the pattern set in Charlie Paynter's days as trainer. No cards! Everyone thought the players would walk out. Well, it didn't work out that way. Some of the players even thanked Charlie and admitted his attitude was right.

The Paynter edict was: 'Be a gentleman off the field and clean play and all that is good in football will follow.' He would not tolerate dirty play in any form and, although West Ham had one or two hard cases in those early days, Charlie Paynter managed to control them. He propagated clean play throughout his years at Upton Park – he was known as West Ham's finest ambassador – and his ideals became established for later generations – including the present chairman.

Always try to play football for its own sake, preached Charlie. He stressed the arts of the game to the players. He always praised soccer played in a fair manner.

'This is the tradition of the club, I feel,' says Reg Pratt today. 'We try to be fair-minded in all our dealings on and off the field – as we are brought up to believe and as we feel it.'

West Ham directors insist at Board level on the Paynter ideals being carried out. If a West Ham player shows any tendency in the wrong direction – I hesitate to suggest that a Hammers' player could

Reg Pratt (*foreground*) pictured with his fellow directors and staff. 'I'm a soccer square,' says Pratt.

be guilty of dirty play – the directors express their disapproval to the manager and ask him to have a word with the offender.

'We don't like any suggestion of dirty play,' Reg Pratt told me. 'So far as our image on the field goes – this is something we want to protect.'

Would that there were more West Hams on the soccer scene. Over the years players have been studied with a view to signing, but have been turned down because they have failed to come up to the standards required for wearing a West Ham shirt.

There has been criticism because another club has signed a player with whom West Ham have been linked, but always there was a reason. Perhaps an indiscretion in the heat of the moment. Perhaps a defect in character off the field. West Ham set high store by character when they choose a player to set before their Upton Park fans.

Another simple solution for selection is that West Ham have a manager who is imbued with the same feelings for the game as the directors, and for Charlie Paynter's high ideals. I obviously wasn't the first person to preach: Let them all play the West Ham way.

Ron Greenwood was appointed eight years ago because he had this West Ham sense of what is correct and right in soccer. He believes in clean play and an attractive style.

'I personally feel that winning the Fair Play award was the finest award we have ever won,' says Reg Pratt. 'It was a marvellous achievement in these days of fierce competition, when to win at all costs is the theme and to get into Europe is the ultimate in ambition for most.'

Reg Pratt, who took Will Cearns' place on the Football Combination and has been President of the competition for the past eight years, has a better ambition than a return to Europe for the Hammers – a League championship title win.

'That is the prize of all prizes,' he enthuses. 'The test of supreme consistency in the toughest competition in the world. You can win a Cup in six games – the League . . . that takes 42 matches.'

There was a time in Reg Pratt's earlier days as a director when the accusation was levelled at West Ham: 'They don't want to win promotion to the First Division.'

That took some living down. So did the accusation that the club forfeited ambition by selling good players. It was a long process to get the fans to appreciate what the club was trying to do in the way of entertainment and progress. A pattern evolved. It became established that you could go to Upton Park and see a clean, sporting game. Very likely an entertaining game. But West Ham were dubbed the Gay Deceivers of soccer for decades.

Reg Pratt, pictured in his Upton Park office with actor Warren Mitchell, alias Alf Garnett, during the filming of one of the B.B.C.'s comedy shows in the 'Till Death do us Part' series.

Following their demotion to the Second Division in 1932 the legend built up that the Hammers did not want to win promotion. That they were happy to be a side pressing at the top of the Second Division. Not true, of course, but it stuck.

The crowd criticised the departures of Len Goulden, Harry Hooper and Eric ('Rabbit') Parsons. The fans reckoned that they were the best players and that, in the words of Reg Pratt, 'all the club was interested in was flogging the good players'.

It was impossible to explain the background to every outgoing deal, but the club got enormous postbags, mainly critical, after each transfer. 'If 20,000 fans had the chance to pick the team there is every likelihood that we would get 20,000 different teams,' summarises Reg Pratt.

The sale of Noel Cantwell to Manchester United created a furore – since then the crowd has come to realise that there is purpose and ambition at Upton Park.

'We have never been a wealthy club,' says Reg Pratt. 'We have kept our heads above water and managed to balance the books. The sale of Eric Parsons was my first transfer deal. With the £21,000 we received we got seven players.

Since the advent of Ron Greenwood, West Ham have shown their true policy of team building and the criticism has stopped. Years of planning have borne fruition.

The motivation for the success West Ham have achieved in recent years began when the Board decreed an all-out youth policy. A booklet, *Soccer at Upton Park*, was issued in a bid to combat the poaching of East End star material by other League clubs.

'We wouldn't go in for the bribing that went on but, as we wanted the best players, we decided to create an image for youth soccer,' says Reg Pratt. 'The youth section was properly organised and started in a positive way with a youth manager and recognised coaches. We began to mould our own players and through time came the players you know about – the stars of today.'

Only four of the current Upton Park staff arrived by way of transfer, Bobby Ferguson, Billy Bonds, Alan Stephenson and John Cushley. The Hammers showed their ambition to compete with the wealthiest of clubs by signing Ferguson, Bonds and Stephenson, but they already had a fine nucleus of a side thrown up by their youth policy.

'There is something at Upton Park for us to build on,' says Reg Pratt.

Ron Greenwood signed Johnny Byrne from Crystal Palace to

provide the main link in attack for the emerging youngsters. 'He did a wonderful job and made a lot of those boys,' says Reg Pratt.

In defence they had Bobby Moore as a bulwark. Add Byrne up front and ingredients were provided for the Cup successes of the mid-1960s. It is a startling fact that Moore, at 28, is today the senior member of the side – it seems only the other day that he was an up-and-coming star of the youth set-up. West Ham patiently developed their youngsters and an appreciative crowd now realises the importance of the youth set-up. Upton Park is the one ground in the south that can 'sell' youth football. The young Hammers get the best support because the fans want to see the latest crop of would-be Bobby Moores, Geoff Hursts and Martin Peters.

England's World Cup trio are all products of the thriving youth policy. All benefited from growing up together in a West Ham coaching atmosphere. Nowadays youngsters queue to join West Ham – a far cry from the not-too-distant days when they sought recognition with other London clubs.

The Hammers can now afford to be ultra-selective and the policy is to choose youngsters with a flair for making the grade. Attitude and intelligence to tuition are all-important factors and, unless a boy measures up in all aspects, he will not get a chance at Upton Park. West Ham do their utmost to prevent a boy finishing on the soccer scrapheap at an early age.

Competition is keen, but the fact is that West Ham discard few of the boys they choose. The club feels responsible to a youngster coming into the game and a boy is given every chance.

Chairman Reg Pratt and his fellow directors take a personal interest in the well-being of the youngest and the humblest member of the West Ham 'family'.

Mr. Pratt acknowledges his debt to supporters, too, by replying to all letters – even the abusive type that followed the shock Cup defeat at Mansfield earlier this year. He reasons that someone who bothers to sit down and air his feelings must be a supporter and, unless the letter writer is obscene or anonymous, he gets a reply.

I have explained, I trust, that being a director of West Ham is not a sinecure. The Board has sanctioned more than £300,000 on ground improvements in the past ten years, an involvement that is to their ever-lasting credit.

Mr. Pratt and his Board try to divide the West Ham financial commitments between the playing side and the ground, and have tried to keep faith with supporters by providing better amenities and accommodation as well as new faces in the team.

The first real security was being able to buy the freehold of the ground – then came the financial rewards from winning the F.A. Cup and the European Cup Winners' Cup. This provided financial impetus and set the club firmly on its feet. The success on the field was reflected in support. Gates rose and the revenue account settled on a good footing.

Although a record fee for a goalkeeper was paid for Ferguson, plus £80,000 for Stephenson and £47,500 for Billy Bonds, transfer dealings in manager Greenwood's era balance. The sale of Brian Dear to Fulham last February meant that about £350,000 had been collected to balance the outlay on players.

The Hammers have plans for further extension of their compact ground, to the south bank end. They may not materialise for five years, but the outline has been struck and planning permission could be sought in the months ahead when the time is right. That would be the last extension – and West Ham could really feel they could look their League neighbours squarely in the eyes with a stadium to match any for care and attention.

Can the Hammers compete at the best level in soccer alongside the wealthy First Division giants? Chairman Pratt gives a firm 'Yes' in reply to the question.

The signings of Stephenson, Ferguson and Bonds – plus that of Byrne earlier on – proves the ability of the club to compete in a spiralling transfer market. And with a 40,000-plus capacity ground – that's what it is today – West Ham are comfortably able to accommodate most of the financial commitment. That's why Reg Pratt is not sorry West Ham's ground is on the small side compared to many.

These days the trend is towards a reduction in capacity, with clubs seeking to provide more seats. West Ham feel their ground is a happy medium.

'It's a happy sized ground,' is chairman Pratt's instantly recognisable description of Upton Park. 'It is compact and fits the part of London in which we are situated. We need a smaller staff than most clubs to operate Upton Park.'

In their worst days the Hammers averaged just under 20,000 people per home match. Promotion from the Second Division brought an increase to 24,000. The first year back in the First Division brought a rise to 28,500. Last season West Ham averaged 30,000. There is genuine satisfaction with the gates at Upton Park – and the directors have a feeling that genuine support of this type merits reward in ground or team improvement.

I asked Reg Pratt to list the moments of greatest excitement in

Reg Pratt – 'We shall follow our ideals to the bitter end.'

his years of supporting the Hammers from the terraces or the directors' box. What were his biggest rewards for the time and energy he has consumed in West Ham interests?

He listed the win at Middlesbrough in 1958 that ensured promotion to the First Division after 26 years in the wilderness.

'I went a bit potty at Ayresome Park that afternoon,' recalls this normally staid and controlled chairman. 'We had been living with that image that we didn't want promotion for so long – this game meant that we could nail that lie. We had been top of the Second Division since Christmas and I was determined that we were going to be the champions. Our win at Middlesbrough put the seal on it. I burst momentarily when I realised that my first dream in soccer had come true. We had been working for it relentlessly – had never given up thinking that we were First Division.

'I know it sounds trite, but we had always felt that we could express ourselves better in the First Division. I was never afraid of being in the top sphere. We had always tried to maintain First Division standards at Upton Park.'

Ten minutes from the end of that memorable game at Middlesbrough, with the Hammers leading 3–0, chairman Pratt grabbed Ted Fenton, then the manager, and repeated over and over again: 'We're there, we're there.' He threw his hat high into the air at the final whistle – and hundreds of happy fans greeted the team when their train arrived back in London that night and 'Bubbles' sounded merrily from hoarse voices.

Quite a highlight to savour. Reg Pratt also nominates the semi-final victory against Manchester United that took the Hammers to Wembley in 1964. Winning the Cup by beating Preston was a passport to Europe – the victory against United . . . Well, that was a triumph for the way of West Ham life.

The Cup Winners' Cup success was another highlight of Reg Pratt's career – memorable, one of those occasions when everything was right.

The compensations outweigh the kicks in soccer by a short head. Mr. Pratt reasons that the longer one is in football the more philosophical one becomes. A sense of proportion is an essential.

He refuses to acknowledge a really black period in his years with the club and admits that, even when the relegation shadows crept up Green Street a couple of years ago, he never believed it could happen to the Hammers.

There's touching faith in an ideal. But what of the future? Let's ignore that dread word 'relegation' and revert to thoughts of the Hammers' achieving Reg Pratt's ambition of a League title win. Can they do it?

'I feel we need an extra bit of concentration on top of all that we have to offer, says the West Ham chairman.

'We have missed so many goals, possibly through sudden lapses of concentration. We've got to make our finishing more bloody-minded. That's all we seem to lack.'

There is no doubt in Reg Pratt's mind (or any sane soccer citizen come to that) that West Ham have the skill to achieve success. They can score goals.

'We can hold our own,' he says.

Reg Pratt grew up with an interest in all games. Golf is his main sporting pastime these days, but he retains an interest in Wanstead Cricket Club, the team he played for 40 years ago, as President.

I support his principles of fair play. Like him I am a 'square' when it comes to opposing a win-at-all-costs attitude. I'd love the Hammers to win the League title – under their own playing terms.

The day it happens that well-controlled Mr. Pratt will again 'burst' momentarily. For it will be a victory for the ideals Charlie Paynter set down six decades and more ago – ideals carried on by the chairman as head of the West Ham 'family'.

A Player's Player

He is called 'Ticker' by his team-mates and the fans for the simple reason that he is the player who has made West Ham tick.

It is the finest compliment that could be paid to dark-haired Ron Boyce, a keen student of soccer and a player with the ability to 'read' a game.

Boyce hugs few headlines and has been described as the 'engine room' of the West Ham sides of the 1960s. Suffice to say, headlines or no, that the Hammers could not have achieved the success they have had without the unselfish contribution of 'Ticker'.

I have known Ron, a quiet, unassuming professional, since his early days at Upton Park and have no hesitation in dubbing him as a typical West Ham product.

For a start, he has never been booked by a referee in a professional career spanning nine years. He has been brought up the West Ham way and is a firm believer in all that is good in football.

He describes his feelings in simple terms: 'West Ham is my way of life. It means everything to me, apart from soccer being my living.'

'Ticker' Boyce is unspectacular and uncomplicated on and off the field. Again I let him define his football role: 'I go out and for 90 minutes I give of my best.'

Away from the soccer limelight he is a family man and he and his wife, Dawn, live in a pleasant house at Hornchurch with Gary, aged three, and the 1969 arrival, Anthony.

Ronald William Boyce, to give 'Ticker' his full title, was born at West Ham 26 years ago. The family lived a crowd's roar from Upton Park.

They moved when Ron was two, Mr. Boyce taking a shop at East Ham, the same distance from the West Ham ground in another direction. So, until he married in the summer of 1964, after the F.A. Cup Final defeat of Preston, Ron had never strayed beyond the confines of the strains of 'Bubbles' floating in the air from Upton Park.

Ron is a classic example of a local boy making good. He just *had* to be a supporter of the Hammers, and he just *had* to wear the shirt of his favourite team when it was found that he had footballing ability.

Arsenal wanted him to sign. So did Spurs. And Chelsea. But Ron, who had supported the Hammers from behind the goals since he was a boy, was 'Bubbles' minded.

He first came to local notice as a member of the East Ham schoolboy teams. 'A promising inside-forward,' said the pundits. Then, in his final year at school – 'academically I was useless,' he grins – he progressed to play for London, Essex and – England.

Ron was one of the two East Ham Grammar School choices for the England side, and he played at Wembley (against Scotland), Watford (v. Ireland), Leicester (v. Wales) and in Dublin against Eire.

At wing-half in the England side was Terry Venables, the youngster West Ham hoped to sign before he went to Chelsea and later before he moved to Spurs; Peter Thompson, the England and Liverpool winger; Phil Chisnall, who is now at Southend after playing for Manchester United and Liverpool; and Bert Murray, the Birmingham full-back who started his League career as a Chelsea winger.

Quite a side. 'Ticker' Boyce had few thoughts for his lessons at the time for, as he says, 'My mind was made up what I wanted to do.'

Wally St. Pier, West Ham's talent-finding representative, appeared on the scene at the Boyce household when Ron was 15 and the youngster began to train at Upton Park on Tuesday and Thursday evenings under the expert tuition of such stars as Malcolm Allison and Noel Cantwell.

He paid Arsenal the courtesy of visiting Highbury for a look at the set-up, but his mind was made up anyway. West Ham was, after all, on the doorstep.

As Wally St. Pier puts it: 'What chance did Arsenal have when he had grown up with Bubbles in his ears?'

'Ticker' made his first team debut as an amateur against Millwall in the old Southern Floodlight competition when he was a 16 year old. The date: 13 October 1959. The next landmark was when he signed as a professional in the summer of 1960. Martin Peters, Brian Dear, Geoff Hurst, Mike Beesley, Andy Smillie and John Cartwright were his contemporaries.

Ron Boyce – known as 'Ticker' for the simple reason that he is the player who makes West Ham tick.

Ronnie Boyce – 'West Ham is my way of life' – is back in defence as Bobby Ferguson saves from Chelsea's Charlie Cooke

Ron was groomed as deputy to Welsh international Phil Woosnam, the talented inside-forward who was first choice at Upton Park at the time, and he was still only 17 when he was given the chance of a League debut against Preston at Upton Park, on 22 October 1960.

'I remember hitting the bar with a header, and the crowd were good to me,' he recalls. 'Maybe I was lucky – we won both matches, against Millwall and Preston, when I was first given my chance.'

Johnny Haynes, the Fulham and English skipper at the time, was always a model for young Ron Boyce, but he had a few chances to try and emulate the classic exponent of the defence-splitting pass in his early days.

'At West Ham you are taught a job and I was taught to be an inside-forward,' he says. 'You learn to fill in for the player you replace in any side.'

Ron won England youth international honours and was given his chance by manager Ron Greenwood to claim the inside-right position as his own when Woosnam moved to Aston Villa.

He has taken the chance so well that he has more than 200 League and over 50 Cup appearances to his credit. He won an F.A. Cup Winners' medal in 1964, a European Cup Winners' Cup medal the following year and a Football League Cup runners-up medal 12 months after that.

'Ticker' Boyce has been a regular member of the side. Manager Greenwood has never hesitated to pick him and the fans have accepted him as part of the Upton Park scene. Yet Ron has never taken it for granted that he is in the side to stay.

Ron Greenwood has told me that, at the height of the success in 1964 and in Europe the next year, Ron Boyce remained modest and uncertain. If 14 players were named on a team sheet he would not start changing until he had established that he was one of the chosen eleven.

'I'm a big worrier,' admits Ron. 'I cannot accept that I am in the side every week. Why? It's a case of being a pro., I suppose, part of a life in which nothing is secure. There's little glory in the role I play. You are expected to do a job a certain way and you do it. If you do it well you stay in the team. If you don't you're liable to be out.'

Despite his worrying and sense of insecurity with football, Ron Boyce has rarely been dropped. I can recall only one occasion when another player was preferred to him when he was fully fit for action.

When I accompanied the Hammers on their American trip, Boyce was an emerging star. He did a fine job, content to submerge his personality to the 'name' internationals in the team.

'I felt that West Ham were arriving as a team in America,' Ron has told me. 'We started to think we could achieve things. Playing against Dukla, the famous Czech side, in the American Cup Final was our severest test. Although we lost 2–1 on aggregate we were cheered off the field after both games and called the best British side ever seen in the United States. It was a boost to our confidence.'

The Hammers returned from America to win the Cup and to take Europe by storm in the Cup Winners' Cup trophy. 'Ticker' Boyce's role was recognised by a call to play for Young England against the England international side at Highbury.

Ron Boyce's West Ham epitaph will undoubtedly tag him as the player who scored the Wembley winner against Preston in 1964, the injury-time goal that made the score 3–2 for the Hammers and left all of us 'Bubbles' addicts hoarse with delight.

Ron acknowledges that Wembley winner – one of some mere 20 goals he has scored in his career – as the most important event of his soccer life. Let him relive the moment in his own words: 'Geoff Hurst picked the ball up just inside the Preston half and took it on. He played it out to Peter Brabrook on the right. I started to run to the far post and, when Peter crossed the ball, Budgie Byrne went up and

'Ticker' Boyce as usual in the thick of it. Here he runs in to cover as Bobby Ferguson punches clear from Bobby Tambling (Chelsea).

missed it and I managed to be there at the right time to nod it in.'

It sounds simple put like that but, for those of us at Wembley that day and knowing that two minutes of injury time had already been added to the 90 minutes scheduled time, there can have been few more dramatic moments.

Ron Boyce is also proud of a goal he scored against Sheffield Wednesday at Hillsborough. He took the ball to the by-line, beat a couple of Wednesday defenders as he cut in, dummied to beat Ron Springett, the England and then Wednesday goalkeeper, and placed the ball wide of his diving body into the net.

'That pleased me,' says Ron. 'Mind you, there aren't many goals to choose from – I haven't scored for a couple of years now.'

His predominantly defensive role in the Hammers' line-up – he's a back No. 8 – enables Martin Peters the freedom for this attacking flair and gives Billy Bonds more chance for an adventurous overlap to join the attack. Boyce covers for the pair of them.

I have seen West Ham play some magnificent attacking games in recent years. I have marvelled at their flair and sense of adventure. Their flowing style when they are on song is football poetry as far as I am concerned.

Boyce sweeps past Liverpool right-half Tommy Smith at Upton Park

Which is why I was amazed when 'Ticker' Boyce listed as his favourite match as a Hammer one in which the side were 'under the cosh' and had to fight defensively from start to last.

The game? Against Spartak Sokolovo, of Prague, in the European Cup Winners' Cup in 1965. The Hammers won the first leg at Upton Park 2–0, with John Bond scoring from 30 yards, his first goal for three and a half seasons, and Alan Sealey adding the second.

The Hammers lost the second match 2–1, and manager Ron Greenwood said of their performance: 'I honestly believe no other side in England could have done so well here today.'

John Sissons snatched a goal in 14 minutes to give the Hammers a commanding 3–0 overall lead – the rest of the match was majestic defence and calm discipline as a wall of sky-blue shirts delighted their handful of supporters in a 35,000 partisan crowd by holding out. John Bond conceded a debatable penalty for handball, but the Czechs could not get their second goal until right on time. Ron Boyce, in the role of sweeper behind the defence, was magnificent that day.

'I really enjoyed that Spartak game in Czechoslovakia,' he says. 'Playing behind the line suits me and I regard that as the best game I have ever played. The Cup Winners' Cup Final was a magnificent

Boyce of West Ham looks as though he is shooting past Ferguson, his own goalkeeper, but is in fact clearing from the Arsenal forwards.

spectacle, but I had a better match that day in Czechoslovakia.'

Ron is full of admiration for manager Ron Greenwood, the man who gave him his chance to make the grade as a League player. 'He knows everything and is a fine coach,' he says of his boss.

'Ron Greenwood gave me a chance and gave it to me early. I am glad to say I took it and never really worried about not making the grade.'

That's a surprise for Ron Boyce, the self-confessed worrier, has trouble getting to sleep after every match he plays. He relives every move, good or bad, as he lies in bed after a match.

Ron Boyce, like most good professionals, is a creature of habit, particularly at ritual times before a game. He always observes the same ritual of doing everything in order.

Ron is always first at the ground. He pops chewing gum into his mouth when he gets to the dressing room. He is always first to change – once he knows he is in the team, that is! – and always sits in the same spot. Ron wishes all his team-mates 'good-luck' in turn – then falls in behind skipper Bobby Moore carrying a ball.

He abhors such acts of gamesmanship as time-wasting and attributes the fact that he is never in trouble with referees as much to his West Ham upbringing as to his own mellow character.

Injuries have kept 'Ticker' Boyce on the sidelines on several occasions. He was out of action for five months with a back injury, had shingles – 'I suppose that came through my worrying,' he says – and a broken foot. He is a bad watcher of football. 'I mope about when I cannot play. It's murder just watching,' he says.

That back injury almost put Ron Boyce out of football. It is a little known fact that there were grave doubts whether he would play again. 'Touch and go' is how Ron describes it. The late Bill Jenkins, the club's physiotherapist, was a great help in curing Ron and ending the doubts. 'I was fortunate to play again,' says Ron.

He plans to stay in soccer in some capacity when his playing days are over and has already attended coaching courses. He has no outside interests, believing that football demands all his time at the moment.

Alan Ball, the Everton and England inside-forward dynamo, is the player who has given him most bother in his career – 'he's a livewire and I wouldn't like to play against him every week', he says.

'Ticker' prefers playing on the bigger grounds of the Football League such as Sheffield Wednesday or Chelsea because he feels the Hammers can express themselves better there. He has no complaints against Upton Park or the home fans – 'I haven't had a lot of stick.'

Ron Boyce gets little fan mail. Perhaps it's because he is an accepted part of the scene and lacks the glamour or box-office appeal of some of his colleagues. But the Hammers' World Cup trio, Bobby Moore, Geoff Hurst and Martin Peters, all acknowledge their debt to 'Ticker' Boyce, an integral member of the side.

Ron is West Ham-minded. His upbringing is such that it is hard to envisage him playing in any other side or in any other way.

'Perhaps we lack grit and determination when it comes to taking the big honours,' he says. 'We have certainly been accused of lacking the killer instinct of some of the top sides – but it is hard to play with devil as well when you play football the way we play and the way we believe.'

Ron Boyce will go on playing the West Ham way. He will continue to be a manager's delight, the backroom worker who does not hog the limelight. A players' player. Even a referee's favourite.

Long may West Ham tick the Ron Boyce way.

Recalling the Great Old-Timers

Football followers of all generations love to wander down memory lane. They love to soak up the folklore of their particular club and to recount tales of the 'good old days'.

Memory lends enchantment. How often, at all levels, have we studied players through boyish eyes, but recalled them in later years as if they were almost intimate acquaintances?

Geoff Hurst will stay on record in the mind's eye of all supporters of the Hammers as one of the top players to have worn the claret and blue. Yes, even by those supporters who gave him 'stick' before he became a World Cup hero!

Mr. L. F. Holliday, a West Ham supporter for 50 years, wrote from Fowey, Cornwall, after my previous book on the Hammers to recall, 'I can remember when Vic Watson was struggling in the reserves, badly barracked and nicknamed "Mother Watson". But he persevered and eventually became the star that he was.'

A star indeed. Vic made 462 League appearances for West Ham between 1920 and 1935 and scored a record 306 goals. He got 41 from centre-forward in the 1929–30 season, six against Leeds United in a game at Upton Park in February 1929. I bet the barrackers cheered him that day! It's incredible to remember that Vic cost the Hammers £50 from Wellingborough and gave years of devoted service.

Al Read made millions laugh with his football script on radio, but behind the laughter there was more than an element of truth.

We all know the fan on the terraces who moans when a player comes into the side, screams abuse at him during the match – then shouts his head off when the player gets the winning goal.

I think the West Ham crowd one of the best in Britain, knowledgeable, witty and appreciative, but as I write I can hear the supporter who sits just behind the Upton Park Press Box who has a blind spot on Martin Peters. 'Mother Peters' is not in it; Martin

Do you remember them? Back row (*left to right*) – Malcolm Musgrove, Noel Cantwell and Ken Brown. Front row – Andy Nelson and Ernie Gregory. Brown made 386 first team appearances for West Ham and Gregory 383, excluding the war years.

needs a hat-trick a game to stop the flow of derogatory remarks.

Distance enhances the reputations of all players. We look back on a moderate performing reserve of a few years ago and say, 'What about old so-and-so? He wasn't a bad player.'

The Hammers over the years have produced great players. There have been players with skill, those with character and personality. . . those that stood out above the rut and lived on as stars as decade followed decade.

The older citizens around Upton Park talk reverently about Danny Shea, the sharpshooting inside-forward whose pre-World-War-One transfer to Blackburn set us a new record fee of the time of £2,000.

A few years later there was Syd Puddefoot – 'now there was a centre-forward – a grand mover', says Charlie Paynter, the former West Ham manager – and the older fans can recall the sensation when Londoner Puddefoot was transferred to Falkirk for a then phenomenal £5,000. Syd moved on to Blackburn and fittingly finished an outstanding career back at Upton Park in 1932–3, ten years after his move to Scotland.

Puddefoot was the boyhood idol of Ted Fenton, the former West Ham wing-half who succeeded Charlie Paynter as manager, and he has told me, 'Puddefoot was the di Stefano of his time, a complete ball artist.'

The old timers will tell tales of Puddefoot beating four or five defenders in a mazy run, taking the ball up to the goalkeeper, showing it to him and then moving around him with it into the net. Once the ball was over the line Puddefoot would put his foot on it again, bend down and then courteously hand it to the goalkeeper to punt back to the centre.

Between the wars there was Ted Hufton in goal – the debate will long continue between those who saw him at his peak whether he was the greatest of them all – and Len Goulden, the Plaistow-born former schoolboy international who was capped 15 times by England and seemed destined to scheme the Hammers to promotion in 1939–40 when the war intervened. Goulden and Jimmy Ruffell, who made a record 508 appearances between 1920 and 1938, scoring a record 21 from the left-wing one year among his total 164 goals.

Another correspondent, Mr. Arthur L. Norman, wrote to me last year, 'I shall always remember those electrifying runs of Jimmy Ruffell along the left-wing, the cut in and terrific shot from the most acute of angles.'

Memories are made of this. Mr. Norman, who saw the first Second Division match at Upton Park in 1919 just after his release from the Army, writes with due reverence of Vic Watson 'flicking them in with his eyebrows and the ball darting into the net like a snorter' and Ted Hufton, whom he dubs as the greatest goalkeeper.

Both correspondents, Mr. Holliday and Mr. Norman, refer to Bill Cope, the full-back who was in the team early in the 1920s. Mr. Holliday reckons he was a character, often misjudged but, despite a lapse of more than 40 years 'Cope stays in my memory'.

Says Mr. Norman, 'One notable character of those days was captain and full-back, Cope.'

Bill Cope – a name that will conjure memories for older supporters of the Hammers nearly half a century later. His full-back partner was 'Bronco' Burton, tall and slender, but it was the hard-tackling Cope who attracted the cries of the crowd.

More memories . . . Mr. Holliday recalls Sam Chedgzoy and Andy Cunningham guesting for the Hammers in the First World War, and

Syd Puddefoot – the di Stefano of his time, a complete ball artist

Brian Dear – scored five goals in 20 minutes against West Bromwich in 1965

John Dick, the Scottish international who made 324 first team appearances for West Ham

Len Goulden's début at Charlton.

'What a delightful dribbler and class inside-forward,' he reminisces.

Mr. Holliday also mentions another 'character'. Dr. Marshall, the former Glasgow Rangers and Arsenal player who, he says, never quite succeeded with the Hammers.

The record books list a few of the great names and the great teams. The 1923 Cup Final side at Wembley, the team that won the Football League War Cup in 1940, the F.A. Cup winning eleven of 1964 and the side that brought the European Cup Winners' Cup to Upton Park a year later.

Great club men too. Ruffell, 508 appearances. Watson, 462. Then come Big Jim Barrett (442), Ken Brown (386), Ernie Gregory (383 – excluding the war years), John Bond (380), Dick Walker (339 – excluding the war years), Tommy Yews (333), and John Dick (324). There will be a place for Bobby Moore in that list one day – he has already made over 400 Cup and League appearances for the Hammers since 1958.

Don't forget Charlie Bicknell. He made 224 successive appearances for Bradford City before joining West Ham in season 1935–6. He then played in every League match until the end of the 1938–9 season.

Ernie Gregory played every game in 1947–8, 1949–50 and 1952–3.

I have ignored the moderns to a certain extent, but some indication of the popularity of the players of recent years is given by the Hammer of the Year awards from 1958 to these recent favourites: Ken Brown, Malcolm Musgrove, Bobby Moore (three times), Lawrie Leslie, Johnny Byrne, Martin Peters and Geoff Hurst (three times).

How will they compare as time goes on? Will today's generation recall Brian Dear's five goals in 20 minutes against West Bromwich Albion at Upton Park in April 1965, with the same reverence as the old timers recall Vic Watson's six against Leeds?

How will Bobby Ferguson, signed from Kilmarnock in May 1967, for a record fee for a goalkeeper, bear comparison with Ted Hufton and Ernie Gregory in, say, twenty years' time?

Will Johnny Byrne be remembered with as much affection as Len Goulden? He was, after all, the most skilful of all home inside-forwards at his peak with the Hammers. I reckoned him the English di Stefano.

How about Alan Stephenson, signed for a record West Ham fee of £80,000 from Crystal Palace in March 1968? Will he be regarded in later years with the same affection as Big Jim Barrett, Dick Walker or Ken Brown?

Only time will tell. Only John Dick (153) and Geoff Hurst in recent years have topped the century mark of goals for the Hammers. Will they achieve the all time greatness of Vic Watson? I wonder.

A CHARACTER

When the Press and fans talked of Big Jim in those far-off days of soccer in England before the Second World War they referred to Jim Barrett, the mountainous centre-half of West Ham.

I have known footballers who were dubbed 'Big' although they were mere six-foot-tall players. Jim Barrett was BIG – in all senses of the word.

West Ham history is made up of players of personality, flair and character. There can be few who can compete with Big Jim Barrett on each score. He was a big man, with a big personality; and few greater characters have graced the game.

Wally St. Pier, West Ham's chief representative, who was a playing contemporary of Barrett's and his understudy, says of him, 'He was a smashing player. He didn't care – he was always fooling off the pitch.'

The cold statistic in the record book tells the major part of the story: J. Barrett, Snr. (1924–39) – 442 League appearances. Big Jim was not only a character but a fixture, a fixture in days when there were great players and box-office personalities in most sides.

The 'Senior' label is attached to Big Jim for the simple reason that he was joined at Upton Park in the later stages of an illustrious career by his son, also named Jim.

Young Jim – I can't bring myself to call him 'Junior' – is now 39. He was an inside-forward with little of his father's stature or style, but he was a Hammer through and through like his dad. He joined the coaching staff at Upton Park when his playing career ended and now, after a spell at Millwall, is assistant to Les Allen, the Q.P.R. manager.

The Barretts, Senior and Junior, played together in the same West Ham team for a short while after the war, another instance of the remarkable family connections of the Upton Park club.

You take your choice on characters; I plump for Big Jim as my number one of the decades I have been watching the Hammers. You only need to say 'Big Jim' around Upton Park and the rest is superfluous – they know who you mean.

He was a pre-war idol of the fans in the twenties and thirties. His son, who was taken to a West Ham game for the first time when he was a mere babe in arms of three months, has told me, 'I know it is hard to analyse your own dad, but I always felt that he was one of the greatest players to turn out for West Ham.'

Young Jim Barrett (holding ball) coaching members of West Ham's youth team at their Chadwell Heath training headquarters.

Big Jim, who is now 62, played alongside his son in what was technically the 'A' team just after the war, a side playing friendly matches for a year. Big Jim Barrett at centre-half; 15-year-old Jim Barrett at inside-forward.

Mrs. Elsie Barrett watched her husband and son in all their games, home and away. When Big Jim was a regular in the first team she used to travel with Nell Ruffell, Jimmy's wife, and the late Daisy Chalkley, Alf Chalkley's wife.

Mrs. Barrett says, 'My Jim was one of the best of those days. I think he was great. None today can play like him.'

Big Jim was 6ft. 1½ins. tall and weighed between 15 and 15½ stone, although he has been known to touch the 17 stone mark. When that happened he dieted and trained twice a day.

'I have seen him at 17 stone,' says his son, 'but he was always very light on his feet for a big man.'

In Big Jim's young days he attended a school where they did not play football, so he was 'transferred' to another school and graduated to West Ham via the district side. His brother, Fred, was reckoned to be a better player, but although he signed forms for West Ham he did not make the grade.

Big Jim played for England at schoolboy and full international level – although his one England appearance was limited to some four minutes before he was carried off with a cartilage injury.

His son signed for the Hammers in 1945 as a groundstaff boy in the era of Len Goulden, Archie Macaulay and Charlie Bicknell, the pre-war favourites who had returned to Upton Park when hostilities ended.

'I always felt my dad was one of the greatest to play for West Ham,' says Jim, 'although I can remember Tommy Lawton as a 17-year-old scoring three against him, playing for Burnley at Upton Park.'

Big Jim encouraged his son – 'he taught him all he knows,' says Mrs. Barrett – and he passed on the benefit of years of experience. But football talk was taboo in the Barrett household, just as it is in Jim's home these days.

Dick Walker, who succeeded Big Jim as West Ham centre-half, was in the same mould as a player and personality and he, too, learned a lot from Barrett.

Big Jim was an army sergeant in the war and guested for Hartlepools when Fred Westgarth, another famous football character, was the manager. There are many humorous stories told about the liaison of this pair.

Big Jim was a practical joker. He once threw a critical reporter into the bath and, on another occasion when the team was abroad, tied manager Charlie Paynter's shoelaces into knots.

Mrs. Barrett recalls the time Charlie Paynter was waiting at 2.30 a.m. when her husband returned to the hotel – reveille was at 11 p.m.

'He gave them a terrible dressing down, but postponed punishment until after the match,' she says. 'West Ham won 3–0 – all was forgotten.'

Charlie Paynter, of course, was a character in his own right, a man with the ability to lead men. Jim Barrett tells the amusing story of the day he signed for the Hammers and was handed his £10 signing-on fee in 10s. notes. 'It looked more that way,' he says. 'It looked like a fortune.'

Like all West Ham players who served under Charlie Paynter, Jim Barrett remembers him as a 'second father' – despite the fact that his own father was at the club when he joined.

Jim used to shout to his father in the course of a match, 'Give us the ball, Dad.'

I like the story of the day the two Barretts were in a West Ham team due to play a friendly match at Carshalton, Surrey. Big Jim was the skipper of the side and in charge, and he was told that the team coach would be met near the ground and directed from there.

Sure enough, the coach was waved down and they were escorted to the ground and undressed and prepared for the match. As they kicked in, an official came up and said, 'You're West Ham, aren't you?' They were five miles away from the Carshalton ground – and to make matters worse the coach driver had gone to the cinema.

Jim Barrett says, 'We tried to get on to the buses to take us the remainder of the journey – but they were packed with fans going to watch West Ham play!' The game became a 20 minutes each way venture when the Hammers finally arrived.

I am sorry to have to record that Big Jim Barrett has had three brain operations since his playing days and rarely gets out nowadays.

For an active man who was always in the public eye and idolised he found it hard to accept the role of spectator.

But to generation after generation of West Ham supporters the name Big Jim lives on. I don't think his breed are around today – and more's the pity. In my day goalkeepers, centre-halves and centre-forwards were big fellows.

They didn't come as big as Big Jim even then. He was perhaps the most versatile of all West Ham players. He played his first match for the club against Tottenham in 1925 and he actually turned out in a Second Division match during the 1938–9 season.

At the age of 19 Big Jim had played in every position on the field for West Ham, either in the first team or the reserves. His son made 84 League appearances for the club and made representative appearances before transferring to Nottingham Forest at Christmas 1954, after six years at Upton Park.

Big Jim has survived the test of time in retaining his own brand image. I reckon he was one of the greatest – and I thought so at the time!

One of West Ham's happy breed

Geoff Hurst, England's World Cup Final hat-trick hero in 1966 and a £10,000-a-year front rank soccer star, is typical of the breed that has made West Ham front runners in British and European football in the 1960s.

A dedicated professional. A clean-living athlete with the will to win. A family man. A believer in all that is good in soccer.

But Geoff, like the comedian who wants to play Hamlet, has an unfulfilled ambition in the game. As we sat talking in his £17,000 home at Chigwell, Essex, one afternoon earlier this year he told me: 'I don't want to be known as a goalscorer or a poacher. I work and make goals too. A good performance is better for my morale than scoring.'

Geoff, whose puffed out cheeks as he bursts into action symbolise his purpose and spirit, may achieve the recognition he seeks as a football player.

His soccer epitaph, though, will label him quite clearly as the inside-forward in the No. 10 shirt whose goals carried England to triumph in that momentous World Cup Final against West Germany.

I have known Geoff since he was an up-and-coming young hopeful wing-half on the Upton Park staff and know that the way to the top of the soccer tree has not been easy for him.

Yet part of his apprenticeship was to shrug off the boos and jeers of the fans who now idolise him. Geoff tells the story in a simple four-word sentence: 'I took some stick', but that tells a fraction of the story.

As his wife, Judith, recalls, 'It was so bad at times that I dreaded Geoff getting the ball.'

Sitting in the stand at Upton Park and hearing derogatory remarks about Geoff meant complete involvement for Judith, whose loyalty resulted in several verbal clashes with his critics, and it is a tribute to the couple that they can look back on the period and see it in true perspective.

'I am a better player for it,' says Geoff, 'but it took me a long time to ram the words down their throats.'

From jeers to cheers. Geoff Hurst survived the obstacles of a schoolmaster who told Wally St. Pier, West Ham's chief representative, 'He'll never make a player', and an indifferent trial game, to reach the heights.

His birthplace was Ashton-under-Lyne. He lived there for the first five years of his life. His father was a soccer professional with Chelmsford, Oldham, Rochdale and Bristol Rovers.

Charles Hurst was a centre- or wing-half – 'a short, determined man who often joked, "if you can't head the ball, head the man" ' says Geoff.

A friend of the family wrote to Upton Park for a trial for young Geoffrey Hurst, who played for Chelmsford and Essex schoolboys but gained few representative honours.

Wally St. Pier recalls Geoff as a big, strong, if ungainly wing-half in the Chelmsford boys' side, but he liked what he saw. Geoff – 'a wing-half who liked scoring goals' is his own pen-picture – was invited to play for West Ham Colts.

'It is frightening to recall that your future can depend on a game when you are so raw,' is how Geoff recalls his first game in West Ham colours.

But West Ham saw potential beyond one appearance and eventually young Hurst – 'I was no schoolboy wonder' – was signed for the ground-staff. Maybe it was his ability in converting penalties that impressed – he was a sure shot with a spot kick in those days too.

Although, by his own admission, he was nothing out of the ordinary as a player at that stage of his career, Hurst had unbounding confidence. 'I never felt I was going to fail,' he has told me. 'I always felt I was going to do better than those in the first team at the time.'

He won six England youth caps and collected a runners-up medal in the F.A. Youth Cup in 1959, the year he was signed on by the Hammers. In that decade since the landmarks have been:

15 December, 1958, first XI début v. Fulham in the Southern Floodlight Cup.

February, 1960, League début v. Nottingham Forest.

1963, top scorer of the summer International Soccer League tournament in America.

1964, F.A. Cup Winners' medal.

1965, European Cup Winners' Cup medal.

1966, Football League Cup runners-up medal.

1965–6, and

1966–7, Hammer of the Year.

Geoff has played well over 300 games in League and Cup for the Hammers, and has topped the century mark in First Division goals. He scored nine goals in ten matches in that 1963 American tournament, a competition I have dubbed as the birth of an era for West Ham and certainly, in my mind, the birth of Geoff Hurst as a marksman of the top calibre.

He won four England Under-23 caps and made one appearance for the Football League before his selection for the national side in 1965–6, the season he carved a niche in soccer history as the only player to score three goals in a World Cup Final.

A decade of highlights and disappointments. A ten-year period of great games and great goals. Yet, strangely, Geoff is hazy on dates and line-ups and, as we sifted through newspaper cuttings at his home, he admitted: 'You know, I can't remember playing with players like Phil Woosnam, John Bond, Noel Cantwell and so on.'

Bond and Cantwell were team-mates of Hurst the day he made his League début against Forest, as forwards. Manager Ted Fenton reshuffled the side to bring the famous fall back pair into attack.

Bobby Moore, Tony Scott, Mike Beesley, Derek Woodley, Andy Smillie and Jack Burkett were youth team contemporaries of Hurst. He came into the League team in the era of Lawrie Leslie, Andy Malcolm and Ken Brown, and treasures a cutting of Peter Brabrook's first game in the claret and blue after his £35,000 transfer from Chelsea that tells of the Hammers' 'cash register attack' – Brabrook, Woosnam, Byrne, Hurst and Musgrove.

'As a product of the youth side I must have moved into the £20,000 class that day,' he smiles.

Today Hurst is in the £200,000-plus class. Top clubs would pay West Ham a record fee for a player who is 27 this year (his birthday is on 8 December) – if the thought of selling ever arose.

One of the nicest soccer stories of recent years concerns Geoff

Hurst signing a new contract with the Hammers in 1967. Geoff signed on for six years . . . and the amazing fact is that he signed without knowing how much he was to be paid. The story typifies the genuine qualities of this tall, strong, skilful striker, whose main concern is to improve his club and his own play rather than his income.

Manager Ron Greenwood and Hurst discussed the question of a new contract on the way back to London from a tour game in Zurich. A few weeks later Greenwood called Hurst into his office and asked him to put his signature on a blank contract form.

'I trusted him and I trusted West Ham, so I signed,' says Geoff. Just like that. The negotiations were a tribute to both sides . . . and to West Ham's fine name.

Tributes to Hurst have flowed in as he has soared to the top in soccer, but the one I like best concerns Jimmy Hill, when he was manager of Coventry City. Hill took his side to watch the Hammers play, and told the forwards: 'Don't bother with the rest of the game – just concentrate on Geoff Hurst. He is the best finisher in the country.'

That's the same modest Geoff Hurst who played his first reserve match against Leicester at the age of 17 and reckoned the match was played at 'an electric hot pace'.

At the age of 19 he was asked to join England's World Cup squad in training at Roehampton, and in 1963 he stood in for Joe Baker in the England side in a Cup Final eve match against Young England.

Fate plays a large part in soccer as in life. How different might the Hurst story have been if West Germany had not equalised in the dying seconds of the World Cup Final at Wembley and forced extra time? Or if he had not changed from wing-half to inside-forward.

Geoff reckons he would have come through as a wing-half, despite the challenge of Bobby Moore and Co., but admits: 'Things couldn't have been the same.'

It's a thought that must make supporters of the Hammers shudder now, but Geoff reckons he might have joined Crystal Palace as part of the deal that fetched Johnny Byrne to Upton Park. As it was the late Ron Brett joined Palace . . . and Hurst zoomed to stardom alongside Byrne.

'Forwards get the glory,' he says of his switch to an inside-forward role as Ron Greenwood looked for a goal scoring successor to prolific marksman John Dick.

'We were struggling for someone big up front at the time, but after playing in the first game of the season, a 3–1 defeat by Aston Villa,

Geoff Hurst, marksman extraordinary. The only man to score a hat-trick in a World Cup Final.

I was left out. I was unfit because of an overlap between cricket and football that summer. I'd had a bad game in the reserves on the Saturday but, as we were hovering at the foot of the First Division, I was brought in for my first game as an inside-forward against Liverpool on the Monday evening.

'It was a fine night, but my shorts were wet through with perspiration at the end. But I stayed in the team and played 27 games that season.'

Was it foresight on manager Greenwood's part that made Hurst a marksman extraordinary or a pure gamble that came off? 'I couldn't see myself as an inside-forward,' admits Hurst with refreshing candour. 'I couldn't see what was going to happen. I thought to myself that if it didn't go too well I could always go back to wing-half, but I wasn't choosey. It was, after all, a chance to play in the first team.'

Hurst reckons his strength *and* deficiency as a wing-half was in going forward in a bid to score. His shooting and inclination to score were strong points, but he was often so tired when he arrived in goalscoring positions that he did not finish effectively.

Geoff is an all-rounder, good enough to play cricket for Essex, for whom he made his county début as a professional in 1962. A memorable game against Lancashire at Liverpool – '0 and 0 not out, although I was in the team as a batsman,' he jokes.

The calls of soccer made him discard his attempts to become a dual sportsman. 'Cricket was spoiling my football chances and my decision to stop the competition between the games has worked out well for me,' he says.

Being picked for England was the real turning point in the Hurst career, the end of the process of recognition for him.

Geoff told me: 'You dream about playing for your country. I always knew I would play for West Ham, but England – that was as far away as Mars, another planet.

'Of course, it didn't happen overnight. There was a transition in the reaction from the West Ham crowd in 1964, 1965 and 1966 as the goals started to go in for me. I scored seven goals in six ties the year we won the F.A. Cup. Burnley was the only team I did not score against on the way to Wembley.

'I remember that the Chicken Run (the section of the ground where the new stand was built last year) used to accept me. It was the main stand supporters who were slower to turn my way. It was the other way round for Budgie Byrne – he was O.K. by the stand but not so popular with the Chicken Run.

Pop star treatment for Geoff Hurst, as he struggles into the Hendon Hall Hotel, England's North London headquarters, before the World Cup Final in July 1966.

21

'I have learned of fights over me among our own supporters. Some said I could play; others said I couldn't.'

Hurst's switch to inside-forward made him work harder at his game and, although I reckon I saw him emerge towards greatness during the 1963 American tournament, he wasn't happy about his form even when we returned home. I think it was part of his not being accepted as a star who had arrived.

During that following season, as Hammers moved towards Wembley and their F.A. Cup triumph against Preston, the newspaper headlines from the club fell to Bobby Moore, the soccer writers' choice as Footballer of the Year that season, and chatterbox 'Budgie' Byrne.

'I wasn't happy about myself or my form,' recalls Geoff. 'I was disappointed and so was Ron Greenwood. We had a hard tour to America and on the journey home across the Atlantic I complained of being tired and sluggish.

'The Boss wasn't happy with me and I was not really happy with myself until after we had won the Cup.'

Geoff reckons his five years' rise to the top was an apprenticeship that has paid dividends. 'I've had a hard upbringing and it's made me appreciate the better things as they have arrived. My trademark now is goals.'

For someone secure at the top in his field, Geoff Hurst is remarkably uncertain (and realistic I might add) about his future. He knows the day will come when he will have to drop from a £10,000-a-year income and he worries about that day. One positive step in the right direction was to invest money in a dream house but, although he has considered business interests, he has not gone beyond the discussion stage.

'You get used to a certain standard of life, but I look on the black side when I contemplate the future,' he says. 'I want to stay in the game but it is very hard and positions are few and far between.'

He is the possessor of a Football Association preliminary coaching badge and plans a return to the Lilleshall centre to further his soccer knowledge and become more advanced. He has coached schoolboys.

'Although first and foremost I want to stay in football I have got to think of other things. I have explored channels – let's leave it at that for the moment.'

With 'perks' from advertising and television appearances to add

Was it a goal? Geoff Hurst's shot has hit the underside of the cross-bar and come down. Roger Hunt (No. 21) has no doubt the ball was over the line . . . nor has the Russian linesman, and England were 3–2 ahead.

The shot that put Geoff Hurst into the soccer books as the first player to score a hat-trick in a World Cup Final. Hurst's last-minute goal in extra time made it 4–2 and gave England victory against the West Germans.

to his soccer income, Geoff and his wife – they were married on 13 October 1964 – are doing nicely at the moment. Claire Helen is three years old and Joanne Louise arrived on the scene early in 1969.

Football gave Geoff the chance to achieve an ambition, to buy a house with a drive at the front. 'I am not very materialistic,' he says, 'but I always set my heart on a drive at the front.'

Being Geoff Hurst, international footballer, pleases him. He welcomes the recognition, but still takes the same size in hats and has time to sign autographs for the youngest of fans.

His best goal? 'Career-wise it was the goal I scored for England against Argentina in the 1966 World Cup because, if I had not got that one, Jimmy Greaves might have got back into the team.

'But the best goal of my West Ham career. Well, that's a different story and just as easy to choose. The goal I scored against Manchester United in the F.A. Cup semi-final at Hillsborough, Sheffield, in 1964, the goal that made it 3–1 and ensured we were at Wembley. After that things started happening for West Ham and, when that happens, things start happening for me.'

When that happened Geoff forgot his complex about the system that produced star ratings and reckoned he had arrived.

'My yardstick for goals these days is 25 in a season,' he says. 'I scored 25 in 1967–8 – and that was a bad season for me because I was troubled with my back. The previous season I scored 29 in the League – and they are the important goals, those in the First Division.'

Low spot in the Hurst career was during England's pre-World Cup tour in 1966. After selection for the international squad had raised his hopes, he hit a bad patch and had what he describes as his worst game for years against Denmark. Sir Alf Ramsey later told him that his display in that international cost him his place in the first three World Cup ties.

'I was nominated as No. 10 in the England party and Roger Hunt was No. 21,' he says. 'The selection was any two out of three – in the end it was between Jimmy Greaves and I for the spare place. To think that I chose that game against Denmark on tour to turn in my worst game for years and nearly lose the chance of the glory.'

Hurst talking on the Hammers is a subject that makes sweet music to those of us imbued with the principles that make the club tick. Discussing his six-years' contract with West Ham, Geoff explained to me: 'I would rather be successful here than anywhere else. I am happy at the way we play at West Ham and I enjoy my football. I have grown up with most of the players and you live, eat

Bobby Moore, England and West Ham skipper, holds aloft the Jules Rimet Trophy after the 1966 World Cup Final victory against West Germany. But Bobby was one of THREE West Ham players in the victorious side. There's Martin Peters and Geoff Hurst on the left – and they scored all of England's four goals that momentous day.

and sleep football with them. West Ham have always been good to me – money isn't everything when you get a set-up like we have.'

Geoff still queries what is meant by success in soccer. Only eleven clubs of the 92 in the Football League can actually achieve success each season, the First Division champions, the Cup winners, the League Cup winners, plus the eight promoted teams from the Second, Third and Fourth Divisions.

The days when a team finishing sixth in the First Division felt happy at the achievement are long gone. Sixth is also-ran these days – who remembers a runner-up come to that?

I am delighted that Geoff Hurst joins me in seeing success as something a trifle old-fashioned these days.

He asks: 'What *is* success?' And he answers: 'Our crowd is good. They keep turning up in good numbers. We entertain, even if we don't win all the time. At West Ham we develop good players – we had three in the World Cup Final don't forget – and I regard all that as success in soccer. At other clubs managers get fired because they do not achieve a championship or promotion. We always try to play football – and that's one of the most successful things we as footballers can do.'

Geoff Hurst is a Gentleman of Soccer. One of West Ham's happy breed. I hope he goes on entertaining, scoring goals (and proving himself as a player) – and that the ultimate in success caps his endeavours.

I once asked Ron Greenwood what qualities he looked for in a player. The answer: 'The ability to absorb ideas and to improve skills. In general, an intelligent all-round player.

'I look for players with character, men who know how to take knocks – and it takes character to be a Geoff Hurst in the game today.'

That then is Geoff Hurst's greatest quality – character. He has survived a tough apprenticeship and the jeers of the crowd to become one of the greatest West Ham players of this or any other generation.

I hope, for his sake, that he gets his due recognition as an all-round player. I suspect not though.

I know I shall tell my grandchildren: 'He was a great GOAL-SCORER that Geoff Hurst. Hit three goals in a World Cup Final back in 1966. What a shot . . . what a great header of the ball.'

Don't worry, Geoff. At least you will be remembered with affection – by the fans on all sides of the ground.